PATRICK WHITE'S FICTION

PATRICK WHITE'S FICTION

William Walsh

Professor of Commonwealth Literature
The University of Leeds

ROWMAN AND LITTLEFIELD
TOTOWA, NEW JERSEY

First published in 1977 by
George Allen & Unwin Australia Pty Ltd
Cnr Bridge Road and Jersey Street
Hornsby
NSW 2077

© George Allen & Unwin Australia Pty Ltd 1977
Typeset, printed and bound in Australia by Academy Press
Pty. Ltd., Brisbane

First published in the United States 1977
by Rowman and Littlefield, Totowa, New Jersey

ISBN 0-8476-6011-7

CONTENTS

ACKNOWLEDGEMENTS

The author wishes to acknowledge the kind permission given by Patrick White and Eyre & Spottiswoode, Jonathan Cape, George G. Harrap, Routledge and Kegan Paul, and The Viking Press, Inc., to quote from his works.

1 Beginnings

Patrick White comes of an established, land-owning Australian family which was part of that increasingly minor minority, the Australian gentry. This class, at least before the First World War, kept its connections with Britain and it was during a visit of his parents to London in 1912 that White was born in London. He was brought up in Australia but returned to school in Cheltenham at the age of 13. He describes himself as having been 'ironed-out in an English public school' but it appears that he made little mark at the school and it is hard to detect any appreciable influence of it on him, except perhaps in certain externals of speech and dress. After Cheltenham he worked on sheep stations as a jackaroo, a gentleman-apprentice.

He returned to England in 1932 to read Modern Languages at King's College, Cambridge. Presumably it was here that he deepened that acquaintance with Europe and that deep feeling for European literature, music and art which, one senses, lies in the background of his work. He was already writing, novels which were unpublished, and plays which were unperformed, sketches for reviews, and one feeble volume of poems, *The Ploughman and Other Poems*, which was published in Sydney in 1935 and which shows no tang of White at all. The poems are sentimental, dated even when they appeared, and insipidly pale and conventional. His first novel, *Happy Valley*, was published in 1939, his second, *The Living and the Dead*, in 1941. He spent four years in the Royal Air Force in the Middle East, and towards the end of the war a period in Greece. The experience of the Middle East certainly entered his fiction, particularly the short stories, and he found a peculiar attractiveness in Greece, 'not only the perfection of antiquity, but that of nature, and the warmth of human relationships expressed in daily living'.[1]

1

England after the war appeared to him sterile – a feeling
he dramatises in *The Living and the Dead* – and the prospect
of living as a London intellectual unspeakably dreary. He
returned home, therefore, after publishing *The Aunt's Story* in
1948. With a Greek partner, Manoly Lascaris, he farmed near
Sydney, growing flowers and vegetables and breeding dogs and
goats. White, an asthmatic, spent some years 'content with these
activities' and soaking himself in the landscape. His books, which
had received recognition in England and America, received little
in Australia, and most of that was scornful and uncomprehending. He was condemned, for example, by one critic because he
explored a mind, a way of thinking, that was foreign territory
to most Australians,[2] and by another because his characters had
no freedom to grow since they were pushed and pummelled into
predetermined positions,[3] and by the official historian of Australian literature because he was self-consciously sophisticated,
affected, conscientiously unpleasant, and tiresomely reminiscent
of Joyce.[4]

He began, then, to write *The Tree of Man*, and afterwards
Voss. White (an intensely private man who although he has
played a modest part in what he regards as good causes is not
much given to large statements and public noises about himself
or his role in society) was once asked, at a point in time some
twenty years after he had finally settled there, why he had
returned to Australia at all and why he had stayed there. The
real choice for him, as he made clear in the statement in
Australian Letters, had been between Greece and Australia, not
England and Australia, or Paris and Australia. Greece was
impossible because 'even the most genuine resident Hellenophile
accepts automatically the vaguely comic role of Levantine
beachcomber'. The reward when he did come home was 'the
refreshed landscape, which even in its shabbier, remembered
versions has always made a background to my life'. It is his
conviction that only at home could he achieve

> . . .the state of simplicity and humility [which] is the only
> desirable one for artist or for man. While to reach it may
> be impossible, to attempt to do so is imperative. Stripped
> of almost everything that I had considered desirable and
> necessary, I began to try. Writing, which had meant the

practice of an art by a polished mind in civilised surroundings, became a struggle to create completely fresh forms out
of the rocks and sticks of words. I began to see things for
the first time. Even the boredom and frustration presented
avenues for endless exploration; even the ugliness, the bags
and iron of Australian life, acquired a meaning. As for the
cat's cradle of human intercourse, this was necessarily
simplified, often bungled, sometimes touching. Its very
tentativeness can be a reward.[5]

There are two phrases in these remarks which have, the
one a negative and the other a positive, significance for the first
of White's novels to be published, *Happy Valley* (1939). First,
this novel very decidedly does not 'create completely fresh forms
out of the rocks and sticks of words', although one must hasten
to say that that way of putting it has a very peculiar appropriate-
ness for White's later, developed style. Secondly, 'the bags and
iron of Australian life', describes both the substance of the work
and the raw bleakness which emanates from it.

Most contemporary readers will come to *Happy Valley* by
way of White's major works, since the novel has never been
reprinted, presumably at the author's insistence, is almost
unobtainable, and merits attention only because of the writer's
later eminence. Such readers will find its style startlingly different
from the mature manner. The prose is fluent and breathless,
oddly uncertain in its gait, and wholly lacking that self-excavating
and rock-moving force so characteristic of White's full powers,
even in their mannered phases. Here, to give the reader a chance
to judge for himself, is the opening of *Happy Valley*:

> It had stopped snowing. There was a mesh of cloud over
> the fragile blue that sometimes follows snow. The air was
> very cold. In it a hawk lay, listless against the moving cloud,
> magnetised no doubt by some intention still to be revealed.
> But that is beside the point. In fact, the hawk has none
> but a vaguely geographical significance. It happens to be
> in the sky in a necessary spot at a necessary moment, that
> is, at nine o'clock in the morning about twenty miles to
> the south of Moorang, where the railway line dribbled
> silverly out of the mist that lay in the direction of Sydney,
> and dribbled on again into another bank of mist that was

in the south. Moorang was a dull silver in the early morning. There was no snow there, only frost. The frost glittered like a dull knife, over it the drifting white of smoke from a morning train. But to the south, following the trajectory of the hawk up the valley and towards the mountains, everything was white. It was higher here. There was grey slush in the streets of the township of Happy Valley, but the roofs were a pure white, and farther up in the mountains Kambala was almost lost beneath the drift.

Happy Valley extends more or less from Moorang to Kambala, where originally there was gold, and it received its name from the men who came in search of gold, the prospectors who left the train at Moorang and rode out with small equipment and a fund of expectation. They called the place Happy Valley, sometimes with affection, more often in irony. But in time, when the gold at Kambala was exhausted, the name applied, precisely speaking, more to the township than to the valley itself. It is here that we have left the hawk coasting above the grey streets. (p. 9)

The undirected energy of this opening is characteristic of the impression the novel makes. The writer has a general intention and an abstract awareness of what he wants to do, but the effect is more often fudged than achieved. The efforts here to hint at the history and to establish the character of the place – neither of which has any inward effect on the substance of the fiction – combines the qualities of listlessness and self-consciousness. The hawk coasting vaguely above the town is an apt image of the writer's distant relationship with his material. This tale of a set of irremediably mediocre people, their relationships with one another being either tedious or melodramatic, is meant to convey the relentless hatred induced by human contacts in a small town. It is supposed to convey 'an unhealthy subterranean intensity. Which is what made these passions different also from the hatred between man and natural phenomena. You know how much to expect from fire or flood. You can't say the same of your fellowmen outwardly united in a small community' (p. 191). But there is nothing Greek, or tragic, or even particularly hateful in the frictions and connections of the dreary inhabitants of Happy Valley, who seem to have been transported directly from some colourless suburb. One feels constantly throughout this novel a very definite discrepancy between the significance the material is capable of generating and the powers the writer is conscious of, but is yet incapable of bringing to bear.

There is not much evidence of such powers in the impulse or the design of the novel. It is indeed particularly deficient in what in his later work is one of the notable marks of Patrick White's art, the presence in each novel of a powerful and creative initiating concept. There is nothing of that kind here except to show Happy Valley and its inhabitants as a minor parish in the country of youthful disillusion. The design is flaccid and without any strong tonic feature to give shape or structure. The consciousness of the novel is not located precisely in any leading figure but distributed with a monotonous equality across the whole.

But White is White, and even in this earliest published work there are clouded glimmers of what was to become so formidable a talent. These are incidental and patchy, a consequence of lack of focus and lack of assurance. They are also matters of detail. He shows even here, for example, the true storyteller's power to rivet the attention even of the most critical and unsympathetic reader. However dim the design of the novel – which begins with the birth of a child (of course a dead one in this context) and ends with a melodramatic death by motor accident – and however unsympathetic the *personae*, tiny explosions power the narrative along, in spite of the intrusive and sometimes quite irrelevant use of a sub-Joycean technique. The streaming of consciousness is perhaps the most inappropriate instrument for displaying and examining a consciousness so sluggish and crude as that exhibited by the characters in this novel. But there are set episodes and some characters who do appear to call on the as yet unrecognised capacities of the writer. For example, White evokes with a strong authenticity the peculiar tranquility of the Chinese members of the community. He is equally successful with the ripe comedy of the stupid banker Belper and his accommodating wife.

One or two of the set pieces are physically exciting as, for example, the race meeting or the later episode in which Sidney Furlow rides her horse, or the scene in the back seat of the cinema between the gross Hagan and the steamy Mrs Moriarty, and best of all is the treatment of the children. These small figures have the vitality of later White creations, and they are seen with that astonishing clarity of the genuine artist which neither smudges individuality nor films it with sentimentality. The children's thoughts, their relations with adults, their volatile feelings, their nimble recovery from disillusion, their utter misery, their strange and tentative communications are brilliantly presented at a level far higher than that achieved with the adults, many of whom are mobile clichés or densely stock figures. White's business in this novel is to show the transformation made in character by a purely disinterested love, but the figures to whom this is supposed to happen – Oliver Halliday, father of a family and sensitive husband of a tubercular wife, and Alys Brown, a quietly eccentric figure of the sort much developed by White in later novels – are both so thin and insubstantial that the reader cannot simply accept them as ground capable of earthquake.

Other critics, while they are not enthusiastic about *Happy Valley*, are not wholly in accord with my view that it, at least judged by the standard of the later work, is an almost unredeemed calamity. Barry Argyle finds that *Happy Valley* 'while remaining for the most part a dull novel. . .shows many of those qualities which, when refined or substantiated by White's increased experience, make the later novels so impressive'.[6] He calls it pretentious but honestly so. R. F. Brissenden reports that in it 'the symbolic implications of the Australian scene are explored awkwardly and tentatively, but with an imaginative power and insight which, though uneven, are undeniably impressive. . .White's description of it [Happy Valley] firmly evoke that air of impermanence which characterises so many out-back towns: collections of tin-roofed buildings which seem haphazardly set down, super-imposed on the landscape rather than organically related to it.'[7] And finally, Geoffrey Dutton comments: 'The structure of the book is taut enough, from the irony of the title to the picture of the Australian mountain town, enclosed by nature, burst open by human beings, to the deaths and destroyed loves which are too honestly unelevating to be called tragedy.'[8] But all see a very distinct advance in the novelist's skill and in the degree of achievement in White's second novel, *The Living and the Dead.*

Happy Valley and *The Living and the Dead* are so different,
the one parochial and enclosed, the other flowing and sophisticated, that they appear to the reader as contrasted training
exercises engaged in by the athlete preparatory to the real thing.
The Living and the Dead is set in the England of *l'entre deux
guerres* and Australia only exists as it might in any purely
English novel, as a stray thought or a possible destination. But
perhaps it required an Australian consciousness, bred in paradisal light, to register with such accuracy and glumness the
peculiarly British colour of the book, which is misty and dove-
grey. No one would want to question the validity of the
Australian experience in *Happy Valley*, no doubt the product
of White's own youthful life working in the snowy mountain
country of New South Wales. But an English critic also has to
report that the touch for the English experience and for the period
in *The Living and the Dead* is extraordinarily deft. White's sense
of the dense and richly loaded presence lurking in the fog of
English life is utterly assured, completely right. The human
article in England was condemned as Henry James said 'to *live*,
on whatever terms, in thickness – instead of being free'.[9] This
was a kind of weather worlds away from the clear, bright, empty
air of *Happy Valley*, and White shows in this novel the kind
of sensibility able both to measure it and evoke it.

It is not surprising that one wants to make literary references
when speaking of *The Living and the Dead*. (The Standishes,
after they leave the country where they stayed as children, live
in Ebury Street.) It is apprentice work and, for all its skill and
sureness in registering with fidelity, it shows clear evidence of
the author's reading, not in the way of reference and quotation
but rather of reading as influence on his sensibility. London
appears as it does in 'The Waste Land':

> Unreal City,
> Under the brown fog of a winter dawn,
> A crowd flowed over London Bridge, so many,
> I had not thought death had undone so many.

Unlike *Happy Valley*, *The Living and the Dead* is impelled by
a powerful leading idea. It dramatises the distinction which
Lawrence made between life and existence: 'A thing isn't life
just because somebody does it. . .it is just existence. . .By life we

mean something that gleams, that has fourth-dimensional quality.'[10] Moreover, it is a novel in which two of the leading characters, Elyot Standish and his sister Eden, come to adulthood in the thirties and it shows, as one would expect of a sensitive product of that period, a certain literary romanticising of the working man, as well as the poetic and spiritual symbolism attributed to the Spanish Civil War. It does this in a highly cultivated and frequently self-conscious idiom. The blend points irresistibly to Bloomsbury. The novel has the silky, slightly pedagogic and culturally superior tone of that particular milieu.

Here is the opening paragraph of *The Living and the Dead*:

> Outside the station, people settled down again to being emotionally commonplace. There was very little to distinguish the individual feature in the flow of faces. Certainly it was night, but even where a wave of neon washed across the human element, it uncovered no particular secret, just the uniform white, square or oblong, tinged for a moment with the feverish tones of red or violet. In the same way his ears took sound, but selected no predominant note out of the confused stream, taxis unsticking their tyres from the wet surface of the street, the rumbling of the buses. All this was so much prevalent, and yet irrelevant sound. Like the drifting faces, a dim surrounding presence, almost dependent on his train of thought for its existence there in the darkness. It was better like this, he felt, escaped only a couple of minutes from the too intimate glimpses, the emotional sharps of the railway platform. It was better to swim in the confused sea that was anybody's London. The personal was eclipsed by Eden's face that last moment on the strip of receding train. (p. 11)

These lines establish in a decidedly defter manner than was the case with the beginning of *Happy Valley*, not only the place – London, the scene – the terminus, the fact – Elyot Standish bidding goodbye to his sister Eden, but also the diffidently analytical quality of Elyot's character and, more important than any of this, the distinction Lawrence called life-existence and White living-dead. Notice the thread of differentiation running through the grey pattern: between the emotionally commonplace outside the station, and something else within; between the flow of faces and the individual feature; between the uniform white and the particular secret; between the predominant note and the confused stream; between the too intimate glimpses and the emotional sharps of the railway platform and the confused sea that was anybody's London; between the personal and the crowd outside Victoria. The reader will also notice the more lissom run of the prose, the quieter and more confident stance of the author, and the greater assurance with which the theme is announced. It may be that the multiple distinctions in this paragraph signal it with a greater degree of explicitness than White would have allowed himself later. But at least this method has the merit of clarity and firmness, just as it has the further value of letting us see the writer growing towards his own more personal and authoritative manner.

The novel, then, begins with a subdued goodbye as Elyot sees off his sister to Spain where her lover, the cabinet maker Joe Barnett, has been killed in the Spanish War. It ends with a modest salute to the future – to Lawrence's life and White's living – almost immediately after this event. The substance of the tale, then, draws out what lies latent in the space between these two moments, or perhaps better, it attempts to realise all that is secretly present in the moment of valediction.

The family context, the crisis of Eden's lover's death, the farewell on the station platform, provide the natural ground from which White can turn smoothly back to the Standishes' Norfolk forebears: to the grandparents, Mr Goose a radical, atheist harness maker, a brooding, absorbed man, with 'square, cracked hands, stained perpetually in the cracks by the dye and polish that he used'; and his wife Mrs Goose, the daughter of an Anglican parson who had married happily out of her caste. Mr Goose raged about the social system and economic lies; Mrs Goose, dim and withdrawn, lived in a simple dream of love of her husband. Their daughter Kitty felt herself excluded from the closed circle of these two lovers. She existed at a distance from these two oblivious beings. When she grew older she graduated from Swinburne, William Morris and Maurice Hewlett to Bernard Shaw and Progressive Thought. She felt herself to be an intellectual, she took part in Fabian meetings, she was pretty with 'enough intelligence for strangers to credit her with more'. She is about to become engaged as the novel begins, to Willie Standish. The scene when she meets Willie's parents is scented with the dry odours of the English class system of the period. Patrick White catches its ineffable whiff perfectly:

> This, said Willy, is Kitty.
>
> He offered it to the room, on to which the door gave, no more at first to the intruder than a suggestion of firelight, and firelight reflected in a silver kettle. There was much silver. Candles in silver candlesticks behind their glass shades.
>
> How do you do, Miss Goose?
>
> It had the high, harsh tone of an Englishwoman defending the formalities. They touched hands. Somewhere another voice, a man's, veering into welcome. She had ceased to exist for herself, for anybody, whether accepting a cup, or giving an answer when asked for one.
>
> Mrs Standish spoke about her sons, of which she had three. They were not so much personalities as her sons. These she had given to the Army, the Navy, and the Law. The Law, who was present, stood with the smile of an elder brother for a younger's indiscretion, and she could feel his smile. It was indulgent, in-the-know. (p. 34)

> The educational system, said the Colonel, stands or falls by discipline. Don't you agree, Miss Goose?
>
> They were waiting, the whole room, pressing in, the walls, the face, the silence politely discouraging. And then she wanted, she had to throw the stone she had held so many hours in her muff, hidden in the clenched and anxious hand, the body rigid in its isolation.
>
> I'm hardly in a position, she said, and she was surprised the way her voice took possession of the room, the way her eye caught, she hoped, the flicker of an eyelid: I can hardly say. The only experience I have comes from the elementary schools.
>
> Oh, said the Colonel. The elementary schools.
>
> Yes, she said. I teach, you know, in the school at Little Swaffham.
>
> Oh, said the Colonel. That's interesting.

> In focus, the room seemed smaller. But her throat was
> dry. (p. 36)

Willie Standish is untroubled by the formidable toughness of his upper-class family and he marries Kitty – 'It happened very tastefully, quietly, with a minimum of Standishes' – who now becomes a different woman, and a different personality, not Kitty Goose but Catherine Standish, and they set up house in Ebury Street. This was close enough to Chelsea for Willie, who in spite of his independence had a distinctly upper-class motive for taking to art: he enjoyed it, it was such fun. White's registration of the tone of upper-class life before the First World War is particularly accurate, as is his ear for its working-class accompaniment, at least in the country. He is less successful later in the novel with a member of the urban working class. The displaced Kitty Goose becomes the slightly frantic, pleasure-loving, vaguely dissatisfied Catherine Standish. Even the two children born to Kitty and Willie take second place to the metropolitan acquaintances, the parties, and the coarsening life of a London set which occupies some uneasy area between the territory of the upper class and a vaguely seedy Bohemia. The people she becomes friends with in this milieu, for example the bloodless Aubrey Silk who 'did not exist except as a number of intellectual enthusiasms' and the hysterically fashionable Maudie Westmacott, faithfully reflect the rootless and attenuated life they, and perhaps their country, are now beginning. White does not intrude at all in these sections. He is concerned primarily with rendering the facts and allowing the characters a proper inward freedom, 'the liberty of the subject', as Henry James called it.

The marriage of Catherine and Willie Standish begins to fail, the war completes their severance, and Mrs Standish enters into that life of superficial intellectualism and sloppy sensuality which is to end in her humiliation, shortly before her death from cancer, at the hands of a particularly crummy saxophonist Wally Collins. It is natural, therefore, for the narrative to narrow its focus and concentrate on the children. If Mrs Standish is a failure, as she undoubtedly is, the children as in *Happy Valley*, are most assuredly a success. Mrs Standish is a technical failure because the labour devoted to her construction persuades the reader that he is to meet a major character. In fact she is a minor one, of the sort which pack the margins of White's later novels. Presumably the elements of life and death, the constituents of 'existence' and 'life', of 'the dead' and 'the living', are supposed to be distributed among the characters, not so as to make them absurdly moral abstractions, but at least in such a way as to appear in different and differentiating proportions. One is not clear, and surely neither is the author, where Mrs Standish stands in this scale. As a young woman she seemed to have the promise of life in her, but her adulthood is either a form of death or an apprenticeship to it. Moreover, she is indelibly conventional, a parcel of fictional clichés, slightly crazy, pretentiously intelligent, anti-bourgeois, difficult, and 'charming'. Mrs Standish brought home pretty and useless objects with the passion of a bower bird:

> Mrs Standish making her room. Mrs Standish sitting in the Louis XV *bergère* she had picked up cheap in the King's Road, cutting a French novel that she probably wouldn't read. . .She went and bought the peacock feathers, she bought the goblet with the silver penny, she bought the little jewelled box that still stood on a corner table, accumulating verdigris where amethysts had been.
>
> I exasperate my children, said Mrs Standish, expectant as a martyr. (pp. 17–18)

And, I am afraid, the reader.

The children, on the other hand – detached Elyot, passionate Eden, and their incontinent little friend Connie Tiarks – are rendered with the utmost ease and conviction. In particular, White communicates the condition of childhood which Henry James wrote about in *The Turn of the Screw* and in *What Maisie Knew*, and of which he said in a letter to Dr Louis Waldstein: 'But ah the exposure indeed, the helpless plasticity of childhood that isn't dear or sacred to *some*body.'[11] The terrors of these children, their separate individualities, their experiences, exciting or desolating, are conveyed with an exquisitely fine sense of actuality. Here, for example, is a snatch of the scene in which Connie leaves the other two children, having to join her mother in London where she is in reduced circumstances:

Goodbye, Connie, Eden screamed. Send me some postcards as well as the letters.

Because parting changes everything. At parting there is sometimes a conscience, there is sometimes none. Eden even felt a sense of loss, watching the receding face of Connie lose its features down the lane. As if some known possession had been taken from her, as if she would no longer be able to keep up a familiar custom. It was like that.

Yes, it was dull when Connie left. Something had been rubbed out of the familiar pattern. A new pattern had to be made. (pp. 103–4)

A succession of impressionistic glimpses and some more sustained set pieces bring the reader to the middle age of Mrs Standish and the young adulthood of Elyot and Eden. In White's treatment of this phase of Mrs Standish's life there is something feline in the accuracy of the pounce and also, perhaps oddly, something self-indulgent in the evocation of her pleasure-loving, ego-concentrated life. We see, on the one hand, her thin and undeveloped relationship with the brittle Aubrey Silk, the texture of whose household effects is richer than that of his dove-grey personality; on the other, the grosser and increasingly hopeless relationship with the rootless Wally Collins, whose only distinction is a kind of rancid vulgarity. Their mother's place as a moral centre both in the book and in the lives of her children is increasingly taken by the Northumbrian maid Julia, who is, in her inarticulate provincial way, a distinctive and successful creation and the forerunner of others in White's fiction who manifest the virtues of plainness, simplicity and decency, like Mrs Godbold in *Riders in the Chariot*, for example. Julia is a beautiful domestic figure of the Dutch kind, 'whether as the young girl, the Flemish primitive that held the baby in her lap, or as the older woman, a comfortable Vermeer' (p. 231). The other character who represents a positive and salutary human generosity is Connie Tiarks, who now lives as companion to an old lady in Kensington. Connie loves Elyot, but Elyot, it appears, is incapable of love. He has a curiously passive relationship with a neurotic girl, Hildegard Fiesel, during his stay in Germany between school and Cambridge. Later, in London, he drifts into a life of attenuated scholarship:

He was making notes on the *Dramatic Works* of Büchner. On the whole people bothered him, the effort, the having to commit yourself, and most of all emotionally. He sometimes shuddered now over the episode of Hildegard. Because this was something over which he had no control. His relationship with Hildegard presented a picture of himself jigging wildly on the end of an invisible rope. (p. 141)

Hildegard is succeeded in Elyot's life by Muriel Raphael, the cool and lacquered ruler of a Bond Street picture gallery, with whom he has a mechanical and staccato relationship, in which he appears more the victim of cruelty than a partner in love. Elyot is only the chief of several characters in *The Living and the Dead* enclosed in solipsistic self-solicitude. Those who have broken through into the world of otherness and reality outside are Julia the maid and the clumsy Connie Tiarks, nourishing her hopeless passion for Elyot. The tension in the novel, such as there is, derives from the effort of Elyot's sister Eden to rupture the envelope of selfishness. In Mrs Standish, the possibilities of life, which certainly stirred in her youth, have been smothered by time and an almost routine corruption; in Elyot they are either sleeping or perhaps hardly conceived; only in Eden are they actively waiting to be born. If, as I suggested, Mrs Standish has been over-prepared by the author for the part she is to play, Eden Standish, on the contrary, is under-prepared: each an example of immaturity in the writer's technique. The only intimations of Eden's strongly positive and creative function in the second part of the book are a flash of rebellion in childhood and an earnest, civic-minded letter to her mother as she leaves school.

Eden's crisis of development falls into two parts, each one a love affair (there is a balance here, a marked, perhaps even an obviously arranged symmetry, between this twofold relationship and her brother's similar double experience with Hildegard Fiesel and Muriel Raphael). The first affair is with a married architect from Putney, 'bland, unseeing, obsessed with his own feelings', a man who mixes sentimentality and sexuality in nauseating proportions. Even the sex is dry and lifeless, 'a chafing of the flesh'. 'She reached out through years, upon her back, through the leaves of trees, and the sound of still, basking water, to the state of physical perfection. Then her hands touched sheets. This then was sex, the rumpled bed, the sense of aching nausea, the dead weight' (p. 147). Inevitably – the passage conveys this sense of inevitability to the reader, not because of some fundamental necessity but because literary convention seems to require it – Eden is abandoned by her married lover, and, of course, she is pregnant. If the first scene of this minor drama is unimpressive, the second in which Eden has an abortion at Mrs Moya Angelotti's villa in Ealing, a house 'no different from those on either side, except that its blankness was arrested by the drooping of an eyelid over the right eye, the pale membrane of a half-drawn blind, either negligent or intentional' (p. 159), is brilliantly successful. The atmosphere of illegal, commercial but not wholly uncaring rescue is established with a ripe comic force (as indeed is the billowing abortionist Mrs Angelotti), while the sense of waste and futility shivers in the air.

White's talent for comedy, by no means the least of his gifts, is more functionally evident in this novel than in *Happy Valley*, particularly in the treatment of the snobberies of the Standish forebears and in the cool dispatch of several of Mrs Standish's contemporaries, and most in the rendering of Catherine Standish's own effectations and pretensions. It is a gift which can be both clinically satirical at the one end or rounded and mellow at the other. Unfortunately, it is this quality of comedy, a symptom surely of active intelligence and control, which is deficient in the phase of the novel devoted to Eden and Joe Barnett. The context of Joe Barnett, his work in old Crick's workshop and his home and neighbours, and particularly the presence of Julia his aunt, is firmly established. But Joe himself is too patently meant to be positive. He is a cabinet maker of the traditional kind. We see him working at old Crick's workshop in the smell of carpenter's glue and shavings, loving the keen grain of wood and the cool steel of chisels, a whole world away from the other tortured and neurotic figures in the book. English life, it is suggested, is now an 'elaborate charade that meant something once, when the figures and gestures were related to enthusiasm' (p. 204). Whereas Joe is much too clearly designed to stand for a new intuitive reality, feeling and life. But Joe is too insubstantial to do more than stand for these things, paradoxically enough, since he is meant to incorporate the workers' virtues in a cerebral and symbolic way. Nor does the love affair between him and Eden, which is planned to contrast in spontaneity and mutuality with the other one-sided and, at the profoundest level, indifferent relationships Eden has had before, have the weight and solidity it needs to be so central a support for the creative idea in the book. It is too calculated, too careful, too dim. Joe's death in Spain is, again, an inevitability which derives from literature rather than from life, that is from the literature of the thirties.

In *The Living and the Dead*, then, we see a talent beginning to assume its true form. The novel has that basic necessity, a strong constitutive idea, which was to become one of the most striking characteristics of White's mature fiction, the presence in each tale of a powerful *donné*, a creative, informing conception. The deficiency in *The Living and the Dead* is that the idea does not successfully breathe through and inform every element in the novel. One is left recognising a distance between the germ and the structure. Again we find in this novel, intermittently perhaps, but still more frequently than in *Happy Valley*, a splendid capacity for the shaped and significant detail. We find, too, the gift for endowing characters with life even though there is a failure here to make them, in the sense which the author obviously intends, representative and illustrative figures. The novel also shows a very much more functional and supple use of the interior monologue and a decidedly poetic gift for imagery. The narrative style is very much more developed, more flowing, and more capable of following with complete fidelity each turn of thought in the author and each movement in the fiction. What one is also very much aware of, however, in this novel is a strong and not always coherent set of literary influences. Joyce has clearly been one such, the Eliot of 'The Waste Land' another, while the tone of the work, sophisticated and a trifle spinsterish on occasion, has, as I have already indicated, its connections with Bloomsbury. And, of course, the idea and substance of the fiction are surely in debt to Lawrence. And not only these but even the idiom of Eden at the most sensitive point of consciousness in the novel is in an accent derived from Lawrence. Here, for example, is Eden talking to Joe Barnett about politics:

Yes, she said. Sick. Sick. Of politics. The political lie.

Her voice reeled. She could feel her own cold sweat. She was becoming something of which she was afraid.

I believe, Joe, but not in the parties of politics, the exchange of one party for another, which isn't any exchange at all. Oh, I can believe, as sure as I can breathe, feel, in the necessity for change. But it's a change from wrong to right, which is nothing to do with category. I can believe in right as passionately as I have it in me to live. This is what I have to express, with you, anyone, with everyone who has the same conviction. But passionately, Joe. We were not born to indifference. Indifference denies all the evidence of life. This is what I want to believe. I want to unite those who have the capacity for living, in any circumstance, and to make it the one circumstance. I want to oppose them to the destroyers, to the dealers in words, to the diseased, to the most fatally diseased – the indifferent. That can be the only order. Without ideological labels. Labels set a limit at once. And there is no limit to man. (pp. 239–40)

This seems to me to be Lawrence not quite caught, Lawrence distorted, Lawrence as an unabsorbed influence. Here, when Eden should above all be voicing the truth the novel is supremely meant to distil, we have a curiously mechanical and imitative jargon.

2 Promise

Patrick White returned to Australia in 1946, first to live on a small property at Castle Hill on the outskirts of Sydney – a district which as it became suburbanised offered to the writer the characters and problems of Sarsaparilla, the fictional suburb where much of his work is set – , and later at Centennial Park, which is closer to the centre of the city. He had already written two plays, *Return to Abyssinia*, which was produced in London in 1947, and *The Ham Funeral* which was staged much later in Adelaide in 1961. White is a writer for whom, like Henry James, the theatre has a strong attraction, and had there been a flourishing theatre in Australia there is no doubt that he would have poured more of his creative strength into the dramatic form. *The Aunt's Story* had also been written before he left England and it was published in 1948.

The Aunt's Story is a many-layered, finely organised structure, rich in material and clean in design. It is the story of the transformation, in the words of the protagonist Theodora Goodman, 'of this thing a spinster which, at best, becomes that institution an aunt' (p. 10). It renders with painful immediacy the process of mental dissolution. It is also the examination of a route to reality which is not cerebral, or traditional, or conventional, or even sane. It shows the solitary spirit utterly stripped and lonely. It is a journey described with the most tearing intensity of feeling to 'that solitary land of the individual experience, in which no fellow footfall is ever heard', as it is put in the epigraph to the novel, taken from Olive Schreiner's strange, neurotic story, *The Story of An African Farm*. It begins with an astonishing assurance and complete authority:

> But old Mrs Goodman did die at last.
> Theodora went into the room where the coffin lay. She

18

moved one hairbrush three inches to the left, and smoothed
the antimacassar on a little Empire prie-dieu that her
mother had brought from Europe. She did all this with some
surprise, as if divorced from her own hands, as if they were
related to the objects bneath them only in the way that two
flies, blowing and blundering in space, are related to a china
and mahogany world. It was all very surprising, the
accomplished as opposed to the contemplated fact. It had
altered the silence of the house. It had altered the room.
This was no longer the bedroom of her mother. It was a
waiting room, which housed the shiny box that contained
a waxwork.

Theodora had told them to close the box before the
arrival of Fanny and Frank, who were not expected till
the afternoon. So the box was closed, even at the expense
of what Fanny would say. She would talk about Last
Glimpses, and cry. She had not lived with Mrs Goodman
in her latter years. From her own house she wrote and spoke
of Dear Mother, making her an idea, just as people will
talk of Democracy or Religion, at a moral distance. But
Theodora was the spinster. She had lived with her mother,
and helped her into her clothes. She came when the voice
called.

At moments she still heard this in the relinquished
room. Her own name spilt stiff and holls dusty horn of
an old phonograph, into the breathless house. So that her
mouth trembled, and her hand, rigid as protesting wood,
on the coffin's yellow lid. (p. 9)

The firmness and productive energy of this beginning are
marks of a new maturity of thought and style. These few lines
are a seed in which the structure of the novel lies complete. They
establish the world, the assumptions, the peculiar logic which
are to rule the fiction. That lopsided 'But old Mrs Goodman
did die at last' makes one's sense of expectancy tingle, at the
same time as it drags slowly behind it the horror of Mrs
Goodman's contest with her cruel opponent. The death of Mrs
Goodman transforms her from the ordering subject to the
discarded object, the waxwork housed in the shiny box. This
process of transformation, of which Mrs Goodman's death was

a model, will be a shaping influence throughout. Now it is the room and the silence which have been altered in a way prefiguring what is to happen to Theodora. *Things*, physical substances, quantities and shapes, are also to be immensely significant. Even in this passage, the hairbrush, the antimacassar, the Empire prie-dieu, solid as they are, project a more than physical significance. The pressure of their presence suggests the peculiarly heightened intensity of Theodora's perceptions, and some disturbing quality in her personality. That tension is exquisitely conveyed in the contrast between 'flies, blowing and blundering in space' – volatility, irrationality, disorder – and the 'china and mahogany world' – the world of coolness and discipline.

The box in the narrative becomes the coffin, which provokes the comment about what her sister Fanny would say, and which therefore leads on, with the fleeting logic of poetry, to the married Fanny and her conventional abstractions, Dear Mother, Democracy, Religion, and the moral distance at which she lives from the kind of reality Theodora knows. But Theodora's life, we realise, was one of colliding with actuality, painfully, immediately: 'She had lived with her mother, and helped her into her clothes. She came when the voice called.' The effect of this victim's life on Theodora is seen in her oddly over-careful rearrangement of the room's furniture and in a subtle sense of disassociation: 'She did all this with some surprise, as if divorced from her own hands. . .'; and it shows in the raw, vulnerable response of Theodora to the memory of the voice and the presence of the coffin, 'So that her mouth trembled, and her hand, rigid as protesting wood, on the coffin's yellow lid'.

The family gathering for Mrs Goodman's funeral enables White to confirm by contrast, in what is a wholly convincing context, the fine-spun, distorting condition of Theodora's nature. She is shown at this moment of her life, when she is living an existence of extreme pain, amidst the squirming Parrott boys with their scabby knees and their round, hard, fierce, animal vitality, their father, the thick-soled Frank – 'a stuffed ram, once functional within his limits, now fixed and glassy for the rest of time' (p. 14) – and Fanny, red, fat, tearful, vain and anxious about possessions. White's management of tone is so skilful that he effects the transition back and forth from the intensity and seriousness with which he seeks to establish the spirituality of Theodora, to the detached and caustic manner of his treatment of Frank and Fanny, without uneasiness in the writing or any jar to the reader. But there is also in this closed, unpromising circle, someone much closer to Theodora, the unpredictable little girl Lou, the shape of whose life had not been fixed. Between Lou and Theodora flowed a current of mysterious sympathy as subtle and significant as the fire which fills the Indian filigree ball Lou rolls across the carpet. It is Lou whom Theodora loves, and the touch of her hands, the positive feeling of her thin bones upon her body, helps to arrest Theodora's sense of melting identity. She also serves a more practical purpose when she asks her aunt to tell her about Meroë, the old family house which is the key to opening out the next phase of the novel's development.

The shape of *The Aunt's Story* follows that three-membered pattern also favoured by White in other novels, in *Voss* for example. The first phase, beginning and ending with Mrs Goodman's death, is a reconstruction of Theodora's life up to middle age: 'A woman of fifty, or not yet, whose eyes burned still under the black hair, which she still frizzed above the forehead in little puffs' (p. 10). The second phase pictures a mind and self burning fiercely away and melting even that ultimate distinction between 'I' and 'otherness'. The third is a concluding, drifting phase of contemplation and detachment.

As a child, Theodora lived in a delicate, if looked at from the outside, but impermeable, if seen from Theodora's point of view, shell of loneliness. She was brought up in the country in an old house 'flat as a biscuit or a child's construction of bricks', known by the exotic name of Meroë, called Rack-an'-Ruin Hollow by knowing neighbours because the family lived grandly, making ostentatious visits to foreign parts by selling off their valuable land. Meroë was 'an honest house' but it had something marred and menacing about it, a quality echoed back from the gnarled aboriginal landscape and the black volcanic hills around it. Her childhood appeared to Theodora as a series of colours: roselight in the morning, green light in her father's book-filled room, black rock and golden stones, green fences and pink and yellow cows, black frost and silver spears in winter. And Theodora herself was sallow.

So that the mirrors began to throw up the sallow Theodora Goodman, which meant who was too yellow. Like her own sash. She went and stood in the mirror at the end of the passage, near the sewing room which was full of threads, and the old mirror was like a green sea in which she swam, patched and spotted with gold light. Light and the ghostly water in the old glass dissolved her bones. The big straw hat with the little yellow buds and the trailing ribbons floated. But the face was the long thin yellow face of Theodora Goodman, who they said was sallow. She turned and destroyed the reflection, more especially the reflection of the eyes, by walking away. They sank into the green water and were lost. (p. 27)

She was awkward with her enamelled, self-centred mother, second fiddle to her pretty, 'normal' sister, and while she had an inarticulate sympathy with her brooding, disappointed father 'who was thick and mysterious as a tree, but also hollow. . .' (p. 25), this never became anything quickening or substantial. There were moments when she seemed about to break out into the world of otherness, or at least to be on the brink of being released from the cell of self, usually with perceptive outsiders who sensed the unusual reality hidden by her gawky oddness. There was the old, but at her mother's bidding a not to be acknowledged, acquaintance of her father, who was not to be allowed in the house but given his dinner on the veranda, or the strange Syrian pedlar who would let fall a torn shawl so that it became a fall of silver water. She had other faint gestures of relationship of this kind with children during her life, with Lou at the beginning of the novel and the boy Zack at the end of it. But in childhood these moments of heightened existence were more often with things or activities than with persons, with the pale grub concealed in the rose, with the rose itself, with music or shooting.

After she had hidden in the garden, she looked at her hands, that were never moved to do the things that Fanny did. But her hands touched, her hands became the shape of rose, she knew it in its utmost intimacy. Or she played the nocturne, as it was never meant, expressing some angular agony that she knew. She knew the extinct hills and the life they had once lived. (p. 30)

(One notices occasionally in this novel, as in the last sentence of this passage, a certain excessive pressing of the manner, so that what was an attempt at grappling with meaning becomes a mannered, biblical sonority. Either this, or on other occasions, as for example in the beginning of the school passage of the novel, the creative effort becomes insufficiently braced and sharp and almost self-indulgent. For example, 'The garden was full of broken music. There were pauses as well as music. The fuchsias trembled like detached notes waiting to bridge the gap between bars' (p. 47).)

At school – and with what acrid accuracy White fixes the linoleum and boiled-rice flavour of the Misses Spofforths' establishment, the several temperaments of the ladies who direct it, and the various affectations of the young women who are being finished there – awkwardness and distance continue to rule Theodora's life. She begins to get used to incomprehension and distaste: 'I shall never overcome the distances, felt Theodora' (p. 51). There is no natural flow of communication between her and others. When the other girls go into the garden in the evening, knitted together by words and arms, Theodora remains behind on the steps. She has a reflecting, romantic attachment to Violet Adams, a girl who loves Tennyson and writes poetry, but it peters out meaninglessly. The grim but perceptive eldest Miss Spofforth, 'solid and unmoved as mahogany' tries to tell Theodora out of her own experience what the girl's life will be like, that 'there will be moments of passing affection through which the opaque world will become transparent' (p. 64), but neither can speak to the other. After school, whether at Meroë before her father dies or in the city afterwards, she becomes a dismissable, eccentric figure: 'The long dark slommacky thing in the striped dress? That is Theodora Goodman' (p. 77). She lives with her mother, individual will and independence draining away:

> You could open the compartments of the house and know, according to the hour, exactly what to find, an old woman grumbling at her combinations or laying out a patience, a young woman offering objects of appeasement, or looking out of the window, or switching off the light. It was better in darkness. Theodora was less conscious of her mother's

eyes. Because when there was nothing left to say, Mrs Goodman could still look. (p. 95)

Humanity, particularly those forms closest to her, relations, friends like Violet Adams or the urbane Huntley Clarkson in later life, failed as the occasion or means of release. What does not fail her, what becomes increasingly the supporting, consistency of her life, is things, objects. Things have a peculiar, sometimes overwhelming, presence for Theodora who feels simultaneously how intimate she is with them and how powerfully charged they are with energy towards her. Things do not, like persons, protect themselves by keeping others at a 'moral distance'. They lie there, full of secret life and ready to be entered into. Human beings crave to know, to include and ingest. For Theodora, this kind of greedy subjectivity is the great monster, self, which, she hopes, will be destroyed, 'and that desirable state achieved, which resembles, one would imagine, nothing more than air or water'. People for Theodora were statues who assumed distant, arbitrary and inimicable positions. Only with things was there a possibility of otherness and liberty from self. At the end of the first part of the novel, after the death of her mother, Theodora sits with her niece Lou, feeling the pressure of the child, slight as paper, on her side, a child who is that mysterious thing, a loving object.

> 'I wish. . .' said Lou.
> 'What do you wish?'
> 'I wish I was you, Aunt Theo.'
> And now Theodora asked why.
> 'Because you know things,' said Lou.
> 'Such as?'
> 'Oh,' she said, 'things.' (p. 136)

As I look back at the first part of this novel, I am very conscious that there has been a notable advance in narrative technique, particularly in the address with which the writer blends several modes of story telling, the description of action, long and sometimes almost langorous passages of introspection, the evocation of atmosphere, and the extraordinary reproduction of a variety of concrete existences. This last is particularly important since it is the means which White has elected both to display Theodora's peculiar temperament and to suggest the strains and distortions in it. There is an almost Hopkins-like power in the way White outlines the shapes and urgently communicates the intrinsic energy of *things*. The novelist gives the impression of having, and certainly shows the capacity of exhibiting, an almost molecular sense of what is going on within objects. Theodora's response to objects, heightened, brooding, increasingly exclusive, is the correlative of her remoteness from persons as well as a symptom of her personal collapse. But we must not take this just to be, what it certainly is, a subtly noted account of a mental crack-up. It is also a moral response, a human reaction. Theodora's rejection of the world of persons is forced upon her not simply by the inadequacy – judged by narrowly rational standards – of her own nature, but by that nature's sense of the selfishness, uncreativeness and philistinism of the world she moves in. Her withdrawal is not merely a psychological but a moral revulsion. It is this which is intimated with exquisite rightness all through this first phase of *The Aunt's Story*. Corresponding to this negation in her life is a positive value, her infatuation with things. In this she shows a kind of knowledge which, White suggests, has its own wisdom. It is neither abstract, nor coherent, nor logical, nor articulated. It is best described as a kind of *becoming* in which, as Coleridge said, there is a 'coincidence of an object and subject'. To know another, in the sense of becoming, was impossible for Theodora in respect of her father, or her family, or her friends. But the possibility of union with things was endless and neither she nor they ever stood back from it. She could become a stick drifting in the water, a rose growing in a garden, music of cello or piano, or the hawk tearing its prey.

> Once the hawk flew down, straight and sure, out of the skeleton forest. He was a little hawk, with a reddish-golden eye, that looked at her as he stood on the sheep's carcass, and coldly tore through the dead wool. The little hawk tore and paused, tore and paused. Soon he would tear through the wool and the maggots and reach the offal in the belly of the sheep. Theodora looked at the hawk. She could not judge his act, because her eye had contracted, it was reddish-gold, and her curved face cut the wind. Death, said Father, lasts for a long time. Like the bones of the sheep that would

lie, and dry, and whiten, and clatter under horses. But the act of the hawk, which she watched, hawk-like, was a moment of shrill beauty that rose above the endlessness of bones. The red eye spoke of worlds that were brief and fierce. (p. 33)

The second part of the novel, *jardin exotique*, is strongly carried on this consistency of things. It begins in a faintly representational way with Theodora sitting in reception at the Hôtel du Midi waited on by Monsieur Durand, but from the first the activity of things and the passivity of Theodora are vigorously emphasised. 'She touched the old dark ugly furniture that had a dark and lingering smell of olives, the same sombre glâre. There is perhaps no more complete a reality than a chair and a table' (p. 141). We see her consciousness not as an organising capacity, but as one totally devoted to the finest and most exquisite registration: 'Smells came in at the door, petrol and oil, fish, sea, and the white, negative smell of dust. A clock ticked, prim and slow, a clock with a fat, yellow, familiar face, removed brutally from somebody's house and exposed to the public hall of a hotel' (p. 142). The objects in Theodora's floating, photographing consciousness, while each has an intense and individual life of its own, do not include any convincing suggestion of an objective universe. They swim in a vaguely moving medium. The system of relations which might connect them to a world that includes more than Theodora is abolished, and the transitions between them are increasingly suppressed. The narrative is packed not only with things but also with persons, but the persons, even when they have a root in rety, increasingly assume the form of projections from Theodora's fnta alisy and take on the glittering faces of things. General Sokolnikov and Madame Rapallo who had settled in years ago, are figures reminiscent of Eliot's Madama Sosostri, the famous clairvoyant, Mrs Equitone, and Mr Eugenides, the Smyrna merchant. They have the same unattached existence, the same mythical status, the same seedy richness, the same icon-like presence. The dazzling activity of objects in this phase of the novel is like the action of a dream and Theodora's state is like a sleep, an abdication of daylight consciousness:

'You must relax, Theodora Goodman,' said Mrs

Rapallo. 'You must relax and float. You will find that figures will evolve, squares, chains, and galops. Sometimes you will place one hand on your hip, sometimes you will feel the hand of your partner in the small of the back. But believe me, the essential is to relax.' (pp. 255-6)

I once thought the *jardin exotique* section of the novel over-extended and sustained for too long on a single note. Re-reading and reflection persuade me to revise that view. Not only is there a more than sufficient degree of variation within the dominant mood, but the whole phase comes as a fitting climax to the first part of the novel, in that the state of madness follows naturally on what has been prepared there. Moreover, this intricate rendering of Theodora's delirious state makes a fine functional contrast with the relaxed sadness of what follows in the final third of the novel. The substance of *jardin exotique* can be described, perhaps in a rather leaden way, as a kaleidoscope of fantastic images. The pieces combine, divide and spin away in brilliant splinters. But one also has to note how subtly White conveys at every point the sense that the agitation is an intrinsic one, and how the hard and glittering passages are each informed by Theodora's suffering and loneliness. In one way the section offers to the reader the incomprehensible opaqueness that the irrational mind presents to the rational. And yet the reader does, because of the empathy and communicating skill of the writer, find it in a significant way intelligible. His reaction to the whole section is illuminated by Coleridge's comment when he asked how a young child could understand a story:

> Reflect on the simple fact of the state of a child's mind while with great delight he reads or listens to the story of Jack and the Bean Stalk! How could this be, if in some sense he did not understand it? Yea, the child does understand each part of it – A, and B, and C; but not ABC=X. He understands it as we all understand our dreams, while we are dreaming, – each shape and incident, or group of shapes and incidents, by itself – unconscious of, and therefore unoffended at, the absence of the logical copula, or the absurdity of the transitions.[1]

Here is a passage from the section, not one of the more

delirious ones, in which we observe the extraordinary sharpness
with which each detail is etched, the suppression of logical
connection, the strange sense of externality on the part of
Theodora, the feeling, too, that every moment and fact is
drenched in her misery, and where the whole can be understood
by us as we understand our dreams while we are dreaming:

> It was perhaps *plus modeste*, but recognisable, from the
> objects she had put there in the morning as a safeguard,
> the darning egg, the dictionary, and the superfluous leather
> writing case. Hearing the fainter slippers of Henriette,
> listening to her own silence form in the small room,
> Theodora loved her sponge. There are moments, she
> admitted, when it is necessary to return to the boxes for
> which we were made. And now the small room was a box
> with paper roses pasted on the sides. Theodora walked
> across the carpet, frayed by similar feet in modest circum-
> stances, with arches that have a tendency to fall, in shoes
> that soon must be mended. She took off a garnet ring which
> had been her mother's but which had changed its ex-
> pression, like most inherited things. She put it on the
> dressing table, inside the handkerchief sachet, which was
> the garnet's place. I am preparing for bed, she saw. But
> in performing this act for the first time, she knew she did
> not really control her bones, and that the curtain of her
> flesh must blow, like walls which are no longer walls. She
> took off one shoe, with its steel buckle and its rather long
> vamp. Standing with it in her hand, her identity became
> uncertain. She looked with sadness at the little hitherto safe
> microcosm of the darning egg and waited for the rose wall
> to fall. (p. 206)

In the final section of the novel, which began in Australia
and continued in Europe, Theodora is discovered drifting across
the Middle West of the United States. The tone here has a
welcome quietness after the hysteria which gradually and
necessarily took possession of the *jardin exotique* section. The
artist has a twofold purpose in this concluding phase: first, to
show the consummation of Theodora's lunacy, and second, to
exhibit her as having arrived, in some other sphere than the
rational, at a total lucidity and complete serenity. She is seen

to possess a lucid and simple wholeness, the condition of the soul, it is intimated, necessary to appreciate the purity of being. Her capacity to experience is now so fine, so immediate, that this is something which is physically present to her: 'Theodora heard the difference between doing and being' (p. 270). Theodora, disordered and insane, is utterly herself, and that self, from which all the elements of conventional identity have been abolished, which in its unalloyed individuality is deeper and more valuable even than reason, is in immediate touch with the world of being itself. 'In the house above the disintegrating world, light and silence ate into the hard, resisting barriers of reason, hinting at some ultimate moment of clear vision' (p. 290).

The character of Theodora – a magnificent creation by an artist not far from the beginning of his career, and the forerunner of others like Miss Hare in *Riders in the Chariot* also gifted with other than rational modes of access to the intensities and significance of existence – calls up an extraordinary passage in a letter written by D. H. Lawrence in 1917.

> The world doesn't matter; you have died sufficiently to know that the world doesn't matter, ultimately. Ultimately, only the other world of pure being matters. One has to be strong enough to have the just sense of values. One sees it in the old sometimes. Old Madame Stepniak was here yesterday. I find in her a beauty infinitely lovelier than the beauty of the young women I know. She has lived and suffered, and taken her place in the realities. Now, neither riches nor rank nor violence matter to her, she *knows* what life consists in, and she never fails in her knowledge.[2]

The novel itself is immensely more powerful and successful than its two predecessors and clearly engages a far greater span of White's gifts. It shows not only the most perceptive insight into neurotic psychology but the confidence and the capacity to deal with a major theme. The weakness in the novel is not in the main character but in the context. There is a tendency – displayed not infrequently in the contrast posed between Theodora and others, for example in her meeting with the conventional, Philistine American on the train – a tendency to take too absolute a line, and to rack the fiction too neatly into the shape of spiritual truth. The writer's hand, used like this in the interest of symbolic truth, is sometimes too clearly and forcefully present. *The Aunt's Story* is a brilliant and daring novel and this deficiency counts more against it than the occasional clumsiness of diction or rioting of imagery. But it is also clear that with it Patrick White has entered into his majority.

On the face of it *The Tree of Man* (1956) is a story of biblical simplicity about a man in the wilderness – but a wilderness which becomes in time a suburb of Sydney – who establishes not just a home but a place, a man who takes a wife and founds a family. The simplicity of the central situation lends itself with perfect naturalness to several interpretations. If Theodora Goodman in *The Aunt's Story* was obsessed with ideals, Stan Parker is the apostle of experience. If Theodora Goodman shows in an excessive way that in every human nature there is a knot or opaqueness inaccessible to others, Stan Parker manifests a nature of complete openness. If she was supremely the creature of indelible individuality, he is above all a representative man. He is one in whom a sturdy, ordinary decency is raised to the level of virtue. There is an uncomplicated and biblical universality, almost of the Old Testament kind, in the nature he is endowed with. And indeed, the novel itself can very fairly be seen as biblically shaped, above all by the themes of creation and redemption. In *The Tree of Man* the novelist's intentions are wholly sunk in the fiction and the reader feels that any of several possible interpretations follow on the experiences and are not imposed upon it. The thick texture in the idiom, in striking contrast with the neurotic fineness of *The Aunt's Story*, is very much in keeping with the centrality and solidity of the common human experience the novel deals with.

The first five chapters of *The Tree of Man* are given over to the creation theme, although that is too passive a way to describe the activity, the force and conviction with which the novel celebrates life, union and beginning. We see Stan Parker, an Australian Adam, in his busy Eden with his nervy, cockney Eve. We feel both the living novelty of the untouched earth, and the force the man turns upon it to make what is impersonal take on the features of humanity. The mythical nature of the context and the relationship of Stan and Amy are treated with a gravity and tenderness which calls up a similar celebration in 'East Coker' where Eliot writes:

In that open field
If you do not come too close, if you do not come too close,
On a summer midnight, you can hear the music
Of the weak pipe and the little drum
And see them dancing around the bonfire
The association of man and woman
In daunsinge, signifying matrimonie –
A dignified and commodious sacrament.
Two and two, necessarye coniunction,
Holding eche other by the hand or the arm
Whiche betokeneth concorde. Round and round the fire
Leaping through the flames, or joined in circles,
Rustically solemn or in rustic laughter
Lifting heavy feet in clumsy shoes,
Earth feet, loam feet, lifted in country mirth
Mirth of those long since under earth
Nourishing the corn. Keeping time,
Keeping the rhythm in their dancing
As in their living in the living seasons

But the novel adds to this epic grandeur the fierce intensity of concreteness White has so great a gift for. Stan is a good man, with the special dignity of those whose work and life is part of the natural rhythm, a peasant, with the country-worker's scabby hands, in a land which has never been subjected to an aristocracy. He is above all a man who lives directly: 'He was no interpreter' (p. 7). He carries the marks and limitations of his life: 'He had driven a mob of skeleton sheep, and a mob of chafing, satin cattle; he had sunk a well in solid rock, and built a house, and killed a pig; he had weighed out the sugar in a country store, and cobbled shoes, and ground knives' (p. 8). But his life was torn between the 'nostalgia of permanence' and the 'fiend of motion'. Amy, born Fibbens, a name which confers the exact nuance of her cockney Australian origins, was one who had had no great affection in her life before Stan. She is quick, strong and narrow. Whereas the man's is a concrete goodness, the immediate expression of a character, the wife is more reflectively self-conscious. There are in her elements of 'the interpreter'. There is a greater discrepancy between herself and her conduct than there is with Stan, and that implies the dispostion, as her relationship with Stan relaxes in time, towards a dreamy romanticism. Here is a passage from the beginning of the novel in which Stan Parker, faced with the power of the bush, turns upon it with a marvellously creative blend of feeling, part sympathy, part domination.

> So they reached their destination, and ate, and slept, and in the morning of frost, beside the ashes of a fire, were faced with the prospect of leading some kind of life. Of making that life purposeful. Of opposing silence and rock and tree. It does not seem possible in a world of frost.
>
> That world was still imprisoned, just as the intentions were, coldly, sulkily. Grass that is sometimes flesh beneath the teeth would have splintered now, sharp as glass. Rocks that might have contracted physically had grown in hostility during the night. The air drank at the warm bodies of birds to swallow them in flight.
>
> But no bird fell.
>
> Instead, they continued to chafe the silence. And the young man, after sighing a good deal, and turning in his bags, in which the crumbs of chaff still tickled and a flea or two kept him company, flung himself into the morning. There was no other way.
>
> But to scrape the ash, but to hew with the whole body as well as axe the gray hunks of fallen wood, but to stamp the blood to life, and the ground thawing took life too, the long ribbons of grass bending and moving in the sun released, the rocks settling into peace of recovered sun, the glug and tumble of water slowly at first, heard again somewhere, the sun climbing ever, with towards it smoke thin but certain that the man made. (p. 10)

As these lines indicate, it is the mythical and hieratic elements in Stan's nature, the notes making for representative anonymity, which are stressed in these early chapters. The land, by the intervention of man, becomes a place; the place supports the family; the family encourages a community. From this point in the novel a more finely individualising technique is applied with the arrival, for example, as neighbours, of the goitred spinster Doll Quigley and her imbecile brother Bub – other sketches in White's galleries of the perceptive handicapped – and Mrs

O'Dowd who is all flabby flesh and mustard speech. These bring
a welcome warmth and homeliness to the solemnity of the novel's
start. These characters, showing a Dickensian prodigality in
creative insight and realisation, are presented with depth and
body. Each offers his own modification of a general human stuff
or force. Such minor characters and others in the novel, Horrie
Bourke, for example, 'a fat old man with veins in his face,
brimming over with the injustice that had been done him', or
Dudley Forsdyke, the powdery solicitor, are in the tradition of the
humours, as it was stamped and modernised by Dickens. They
have each an extraordinary crackle and Australian pun-
gency. They are also peculiarly in place in a novel bent on
exploring the intimations of ordinary life and particularly of the
vitality of ordinary life.

Another influence which begins to appear as a shaping force
in the novel is the tension – the particular kind of original sin
or inherited imperfection in this Eden – which reveals itself
between husband and wife. The husband is totally committed
to the land and its rhythms. He accepts and rejoices in its
harshness and its distance, whereas Amy hates the wind and the
distance and the road, and is jealous of their omnipotence. The
wife is frayed by her consciousness of what she cannot possess,
whether in the forms of nature or in the sensibility of her
husband. She longs for a kind of expression Stan is incapable
of; 'So instead of telling her smooth things, that were not his
anyway, he took her hand over the remnants of their sorry meal.
The bones of his hand were his, and could better express the
poem that was locked inside him and that would never otherwise
be released' (pp. 24–5). By now the paddocks are cleared, the
house, enlarged and improved, stood with some dignity, 'even
pretending a bit beneath the tendrils of vines and a shower of
roses' (p. 109). Stan was one for whom the flow of existence
was sufficient. His bodily action suggested the welcome he gave
to whatever came. 'All was good, almost, that could come to this
pass. The stone leaped and was restrained by the controlling wire.
The strength of his hands shaped the metal. It would have been
possible at such times to shape almost anything into a right shape'
(p. 109).

But the novel does not operate simply on the natural and
psychological plane. The Dickensian tradition, of humours is

complicated by Patrick White's religious respect for the quality
of pure being, so that the possibility of spiritual experience is
latent even in the minor characters. At the same time the natural
world is given a cosmic significance. Besides the tradition of
humours, another and relevant one influences the novel, namely
the tradition of the four elements of nature. The power of the
land is the opening theme; the conclusion is an affirmation of
the continuity of the earth's life: 'So that in the end there were
the trees. The boy walking through them with his head drooping
as he increased in stature. Putting out shoots of green thought.
So that, in the end, there was no end' (p. 499). There are
throughout the novel commanding set pieces on the wind, on
flood, on fire, making together a combination of ancient cos-
mology and biblical drama. The scope of the novel is enlarged
by this cosmic sense which provides the context for the author's
vision of human nature. It is a vision which sees life as a tragedy
that can, possibly, be repaired. Human life includes an intrinsic
limitation, an imperfection which is a sort of unwilled fall.
Suffering is a function of that fall and Stan's life dramatises both
the actuality of the fall in time and place and the possibilities,
also contained in human nature, for healing and redemption. The
redemptive initiative comes from within and is set in train not
by any act of the will but by the condition of simplicity, which
is so notable a mark of Stan's personality.

Just as *The Aunt's Story* showed how neurosis could be the
means to an apprehension fuller than the conventionally 'normal'
one, so *The Tree of Man* shows the capacity of decent ordinariness to be transformed into a higher order of existence altogether.
It requires, of course, a kind of genius, the genius for *becoming*
in Theodora, the genius for *staying* in Stan. There was always
an intrinsic fidelity between Stan's inmost nature and each
manifestation of it. This loyalty, or stubbornness, when it is
complete produces a special human perfection, intensely 'natural'
and in harmony with the rhythm of the land and the weather
and the bases of physical existence which had so much to do
with producing and ripening it. Natural, certainly, in this sense,
and thoroughly human but also fine and capable of development
into a maturity that is truly spiritual.

If Stan's development shows him with a nature profoundly
serene and realist and a capacity for heroic action – as he shows

in the fire at Glastonbury – as a secular saint, Amy's – to me
no less a sympathetic though more complicated character than
Stan – is a more tortured progression. Stan 'was in love with
the rightness of the world' (p. 152). He respected, says White,
he respected and accepted Amy's mysteries, as she could never
respect and accept his. What Amy could not possess became alien
to her, making her sour and strident, causing her husband to
move away from her. 'If she could have held his head in her
hands and looked into the skull at his secret life, whatever it
was, then, she felt, she might have been placated' (p. 150). There
was also in Amy a romantic, dreamy strain, which her life and
environment gave no nourishment to, and which accounts for her
infatuation with Madelaine, a beautiful guest at the home of
the rich ex-businessman Armstrong. Madeleine, a city-like and
substantial figure, becomes the focus of Amy's romanticism as
she rides around the country on a splendid horse. Madeleine is
one of the few hardly realised figures in the novel, more an
unconvincing gesture than a solid creation. At least this is true
in her original *persona*, which is brutally terminated when she
is rescued by Stan from a fire at the Armstrongs' affectedly named
mansion, Glastonbury, with her brilliant hair burnt clean off
her skull. Later, as Mrs Fisher and the companion of Thelma,
Amy's daughter, she is still a thin but a much less literary
creature.

Any sense the reader may have of an author manipulating
his material, such as he finds in places in *The Aunt's Story*, is
wholly absent from his response to *The Tree of Man*. Here the
intention is sunk in the art, the will quite submerged in the fiction.
The author's design is gradually composed by what is latent in
the situation, and it appears in the end with the flawed clarity
and stumbling incoherence which belong to the pattern of a living
art, and which are ultimately much more powerfully convincing
than any application of an *a priori* design. There is a centrality,
a universality, in the original situation and its development; in
the way Stan first appears as the unnamed man, an anonymous
representative of a future race; in the growth of family and
community; in the way in which what is wrong in the original
pair works itself out in the corruption of the children. What is
wrong lies, generally, in the connection of husband and wife;
it is the product – must we not say the inevitable product? –

of any such relationship. But if it is to be located more precisely, it lies in the wife. The husband is a good man, with the special dignity of those whose life and work are part of a more inclusive natural rhythm. He is a peasant, but a peasant in a land which had never known, never been subjected to, an aristocracy. The wife, on the other hand, is a sharper, neater intelligence and has a much higher degree of self-limited interest. The man's is an unaffected, spontaneous goodness, the expression of a style of character and life. His whole being is manifest in every action and relationship. The wife is more reflectively self-conscious; there is a greater discrepancy between herself and her conduct, and that, given her upbringing and background, implies, when she is not pressed by the urgencies of life, a bias towards escapist fantasy, a characteristic which brings about her lapse into sensuality and infidelity. Concupiscence in her case is as much a matter of discontent as of passion. It is provoked by the romanticism which is part of her nature and which contrasts with the strong and humble realism of her husband. *Her* romanticism becomes enfeebled in her daughter into the exquisitely ugly cult of Australian gentility. *His* realism becomes in his son, where it is uninformed by the kind of sanity which places one in a larger, more permanent scheme, the realism of power, which in the boy's situation means petty crime and the more sordid kinds of delinquency.

After the war, in middle life, a kind of remoteness develops between Stan and others. Perfectly attuned to, and lyrically delighting in, the natural world – 'He would sit with his hands on the still wheel, till their dried-up skin had disintegrated in the light of sand and grey leaf, so that his body was no longer surprised at the mystery of stillness, of which he was a part' (pp. 244–5) – he grows more solitary and separate from human beings. His neighbours find him queer and tend to avoid him, he is uneasy with his sullen young son Ray, a whining lumpish boy, given to indulging a vein of cruelty, or his self-obsessed daughter Thelma. He eludes the possessiveness of his wife. Stan feels the still, limpid presence of the afflicted Doll Quigley in contrast to his self-absorbed children and his tenderly rapacious wife. He recognises in Doll Quigley that purity of being which he was unable to convert into terms of his own reality. This nature of his thwarted and disturbed his wife and embarrassed

his boy, Ray. The boy now dislikes his father; even his smell
is offensive. Once when they are together in the car the boy slams
out, finding his father's presence intolerable.

> There was a lizard amongst the stones that the man saw,
> and to which his attention now clung with the hope of the
> hopeless. As if he might suddenly interpret for his son, by
> some divine dispensation, with such miraculous clarity and
> wisdom, the love and wonder the horny lizard had roused
> in him. That day could still become transparent, which
> remained opaque. (pp. 226–7)

The collected wholeness of Stan's nature perplexes and angers
his family and his neighbours.

Stan stubbornly preserves the peculiar autonomy of his
nature against the rubbing of time and the disappearance of the
wilderness, first into the town and then into the suburbs;
preserves in spite of the incomprehension of his wife and of the
grubby decline into delinquency of his bright, callous son and
the rise into pinched gentility of his oppressively neat daughter.
This unity of being, at the centre of which is a strong, humble
realism, seems essentially to be an exquisite matching of self and
experience. As he ages, all things in Stan's eyes become forms
of experience to be contemplated and accepted, not resisted, not
desired or possessed. Even the members of his family take on
this status. White's skill in realising this spiritual growth is
matched by the tact with which he indicates the ageing of Stan:
in the way, for example, in middle age Stan realises – actually
at the point when he is trying to recall his flash of passion for
Madeleine – how 'whole rooms of his mind, in which each
separate detail had been stored, seemed to have gone. . .' (p. 221);
in the stiffening of a knee; in the way Stan's mouth becomes
tight and a bit ironic when he recognises that uprooting a stone,
which he could once have done with a single delighted effort,
now leaves him shattered and gasping; in the transformation of
motion from silky smoothness to something brittle and chalky.

Again, there is a superb technical achievement in the way
in which White confirms Stan's profound inner tranquility,
setting him in a context in which a whole swarm of characters
writhe with vitality: not only the spinster Doll and her imbecile
brother Bub, or Mrs O'Dowd, who figures in what are certainly

two magnificent comic scenes, the quarrel with her husband and her own death, which are told in a sardonic, accurate, immensely funny but wholly unmocking way. Not only these but Dudley Forsdyke, Thelma's husband, who was 'so used to examining reports on living that he had been made drunk suddenly by the smell of life [which] came up at him down the ploughed field and down the wet hill' (p. 351); and Horrie Bourke, the horsetrainer, who had befriended and been swindled by Stan's son Ray:

> He was a fat old man with veins in his face, brimming over with the injustice that had been done him, and afraid that someday, if not soon, even tomorrow, perhaps, he would have a stroke. So that mixed up with the tears that he shed for the son who was not his but might have been, a recipient of presents as well as a giver of them, was hate for the healthy young man, whose muscles were impressive in his singlet, who stood laughing by the dung heap in a sheen of horses, and threatened him callously with a seizure. (p. 277)

The Tree of Man succeeds with quite glittering success in establishing the palpable actuality of common life, and further in communicating the intimations of other realities which lie locked within quotidian experience. Amy is the ordinary 'ordinary' person, a figure drawn with great inwardness of understanding, both of her strengths and limitations. But Amy herself is capable of creative, exotic experiences, whether in her bouts of sensuality with the repulsive salesman or in her intense appreciation of the strange artist, the postmistress's seemingly lunatic husband, and his amazing pictures. Stan is the extraordinary 'ordinary' man, capable of finding miracles and marvels in the habitual run of events, and with a rare gift of persistence, of keeping his integral self whole and intact. Stan is shown, in a way most unusual in White's fiction where the damaged are the possessors of the enlightened consciousness, as the common, central, day-to-day man in whom the modest and usual qualities of goodness rise to the level of true perception. We see this twofold power when just before Stan's death he sits in his chair on the grass on a winter afternoon. He no longer wanted to speak to anyone, 'his eyes had been reduced to a rudimentary shape, from which they observed, you felt, a version of objects that was possibly true' (p. 494). A young revivalist missionary trying to convert the old man from his supposed indifference to salvation tells melodramatic stories of his own dissolute life. *He* had been redeemed. Why not then the old man?

The old man was intensely unhappy.

When the young one had finished his orgasm, he presented the open palms of his hands and told how he had knelt upon his knees, and grace descended on him.

'This can happen to you too,' he said, kneeling on one knee, and sweating at every pore.

The old man cleared his throat. 'I'm not sure whether I am intended to be saved,' he said.

The evangelist smiled with youthful incredulity. No subtleties would escape the steam roller of faith. 'You don't understand,' he said smilingly.

If you can understand, at your age, what I have been struggling with all my life, then it is a miracle, thought the old man.

He spat on the ground in front of him. He had been sitting for some time in one position, and had on his chest a heaviness of phlegm.

'I am too old,' he said colourlessly.

He was tired really. He wanted to be left alone.

'But the glories of salvation,' persisted the evangelist, whose hair went up in even waves, 'these great glories are everybody's for the asking, just by a putting out of the hand.'

The old man fidgeted. He was not saying anything. Great glories were glittering in the afternoon. He had already been a little dazzled.

'You are not stubborn, friend?'

'I would not be here if I was not stubborn,' said the old man.

'Don't you believe in God, perhaps?' asked the evangelist, who had begun to look around him and to feel the necessity for some further stimulus of confession. 'I can show you books,' he yawned.

Then the old man who had been cornered long enough,

saw, through perversity perhaps, but with his own eyes. He was illuminated.

He pointed with his stick at the gob of spittle.

'That is God', he said.

As it lay glittering intensely and personally on the ground.

The young man frowned rather. You met all kinds. (p. 495)

The old man's utterance is not an observation capable of proof or disproof. It is the climax of a life and issues from a hard, worn wisdom. What he sees, and what the gob shares with God, is the quality of pure being.

3 Major Phase I

The novels so far treat of a place, a family, a crazed spinster, a farmer working land he has cleared himself: subjects which develop a whole clutch of a novelist's gifts and manifest not only the increasing scope but also the courage of a most significant talent. *Voss*, the fifth of Patrick White's novels, was published in 1957. It is the first of a line of novels including *Riders in the Chariot*, *The Solid Mandala*, *The Vivisector*, *The Eye of the Storm*, in which qualities of largeness, uninhibited confidence and creative energy are strikingly present. *Voss* is an historical novel set in the 1840s. The germ of the idea was presented to White by contemporary accounts of Leichhardt's expeditions across the Australian continent. It was conceived during the London blitz, was 'influenced by the arch-megalomaniac of the day',[1] Hitler, and developed during months spent trapesing backwards and forwards across the Egyptian and Cyrenaican deserts'.[2] It is the product of years of brooding on the history and significance of his own country. It is also an expression of White's panic at what he saw as the Australian exaltation of the average.

> In all directions stretched the Great Australian Emptiness, in which the mind is the least of possessions, in which the rich man is the important man, in which the schoolmaster and the journalist rule what intellectual roost there is. . .and the march of material ugliness does not raise a quiver from the average nerves.[3]

The Tree of Man burrows into the commonplace; *Voss* reconstructs the extreme. The wilderness which was to be domesticated in *The Tree of Man*, in *Voss* is to school the hero. If we use a biblical analogy, which seems distinctly appropriate to the character of Patrick White's work, we can say that *The*

41

Tree of Man is his version of Adam, and *Voss* his John the Baptist. (But leading to what Christ? the reader may wonder. The answer, if there is an answer, suggested by the novel, seems to be some intrinsic or buried Christ in Voss himself.)

Voss is simply organised into three parts: the preparation for the expedition, the journey in 1845 across the continent itself, and the aftermath which consists of a second minor expedition to investigate the calamity of the original exploration and what follows from it. The first part is a remarkable 'composition' in its own right, which gives me the opportunity to notice a gift of Patrick White's I have not referred to yet, namely his sensitive historical imagination. Nineteenth-century Sydney, an English provincial city set down on the Pacific shore, with its cathedral, barracks and public gardens (a significant collocation), presses its identity upon one. White is engaged with the mercantile part of this society which lives in solid stone houses filled with mahogany furniture, books of sermons, gazeteers and almanacs, desks covered with red tooled leather, pieces of engraved silver, and tightly buttoned, slippery chairs. These merchants are used to fine clothes and rich food, have an almost mystical – certainly a more than economic – absorption in money, are deferential to the local gentry, and both consciously above, and genuinely under an obligation towards, their inferiors. They observe a cramped but genuine moral code and they are especially sensitive about the respectability it earns. Patrick White catches exactly the whiff of this plum-cake world of colonial gentility, strangely surrounded by mysterious gardens full of feathery bamboos, camellia bushes and scurfy native paperbarks. The people are as convincing as the setting. Massed in the middle is the strongly physical presence of the Bonner family, the complacent husband, his comfortable wife, their creamy daughter and her rubicund young officer.

> Wealthy by colonial standards, the merchant had made money in a solid business, out of Irish linens and Swiss muslins, damask, and huckaback, and flannel, green baize, and India twills. The best-quality gold leaf was used to celebrate the name of EDMUND BONNER – ENGLISH DRAPER, and ladies driving down George Street, the wives of officers and graziers, in barouche and brougham, would bow to that

respectable man. Why, on several occasions, he had even been consulted in confidence, he told, by Lady G—, who was so kind as to accept a tablecloth and several pair of linen sheets. (p. 22)

At each end of the scale of intelligence of which the Bonners are, as it were, the norm, are murmurous reminders of different possibilities. At one end is the squat, pregnant maid Rose, whose baby Laura Trevelyan will eventually adopt as her own, an elemental being, close to the animals and the instinctive organic world. At the other is Laura Trevelyan, isolated in her small circle by her cool, 'Cambridge' intelligence and taste for the things of the mind. She meets Voss at a time when she is tortured by the possibility of losing her religious faith. Voss is a totally new experience for her, alien both to her conventional connections and to her own preference for moderate rationality. He was like lightning or inspiration, and inspiration, the uncalled for, the unearthed experience, is important in a novel which is to be devoted in a major way to exploring the pure and abstract will: important, that is, as another possibility or dimension in human experience. The will causes its consequences but 'inspiration descends only in flashes, to clothe circumstances; it is not stored up in a barrel, like salt herrings, to be doled out' (p. 42). Voss, the extraordinary German, affects her like poetry, so that she deserted when she was with him 'that rational level to which she was determined to adhere' (p. 68) and her thoughts became natural and passionate. The passivity of her existence flares into intensity in his presence. She appreciates him in a way that no others in her circle can but she is also still sufficiently 'rational' to understand his nature.

Patrick White is seldom able to keep within the limit of what is strictly necessary to his design. He loves the pure creative play or flourish. And yet by the end of this first movement – not, I think, an inappropriate term – a considerable amount of the work of the novel has been completed and the rest set in train. The dowdy town and the easy country around it, against which the harshness of the desert will be measured, are clearly in the reader's mind: the decent average of the population against which the ferociously extreme nature of Voss can be tested has been established; the relationship of Voss and Laura has been initiated, a relationship which, since they never meet again, is carried on in the imagination of each and opened up to the reader by their correspondence. The members of the group accompanying Voss have been delineated with just that right degree of definition to mark them off as separate persons and yet to keep them united in a single party. Above all the preliminary work on the gigantic figure of Voss is carried firmly through.

We first see Voss – announced by the puzzled maid as 'a kind of foreign gentleman' – squirming in a social encounter with Laura, but it is rapidly borne in on the reader that his unease is not by any means a mere discomfort at unfamiliar modes of decorum. Voss is one whose powers are concentrated with ferocious intensity upon an inner life. The outer world is either a nuisance or a menace: 'All that was external to himself he mistrusted, and was happiest in silence, which is immeasurable, like distance, and the potentialities of self' (p. 24). His general seediness and frayed clothes, his contempt of social niceties, clothe the arrogance of an unnatural confidence. He was capable of simplicity and sincerity although it was very hard for a stranger to recognise these feelings in him. The approach of others was a threat, much more destructive to his personality than thirst or fever or physical exhaustion. The impulse of Voss's actions was not any general belief or idea but the pure shape of the will which has no content – no describable content – only force and direction. The compulsion he felt to cross the continent came from the desire to fulfil his own nature or, more correctly and more narrowly, came from the force of his will. He was placed in a situation in which the conquering of the desert might seem natural to others for reasons of economics or geography or knowledge itself, and Voss is willing to make an outward accommodation to such notions. In reality, for Voss the expedition was a personal wrestling with the continent, the only opponent his pride would acknowledge as adequate. 'Deserts prefer to resist history and develop along their own lines' (p. 67); they have, that is, a natural hostility to submitting to the will of man and they are, therefore, a proper target for Voss's colossal pride.

> 'Yes', answered Voss, without hesitation, 'I will cross the continent from one end to the other. I have every

intention to know it with my heart. Why I am pursued by this necessity, it is no more possible for me to tell than it is for you, who have made my acquaintance only before yesterday.' (p. 36)

In the second phase of the novel two lines of narrative are sustained. In one, the expedition is conducted through more and more difficult, and finally brutal, country towards its disastrous end; in the other the relationship of Voss and Laura is developed in a series of meditations and (unreceived) letters. The two worlds of actuality and possibility are kept in touch and the latter, it is suggested, offers in the end a possibility of salvation to the former. There is a passage at one point in the journey in which this touching of two orders of existence is itself used as an image of the land.

> Over all this scene, which was more a shimmer than the architecture of landscape, palpitated extraordinary butterflies. Nothing had been seen yet to compare with their colours, opening and closing, opening and closing. Indeed, by the addition of this pair of hinges, the world of semblance communicated with the world of dream. (p. 277)

Not only in the architecture of landscape, but also in the architecture of people the two worlds of semblance and dream communicate with each other.

Each member of the party obeys the logic of his own nature and responds to the sufferings of the journey in his own way. But all the physical horrors are subservient to the monstrous, Marlovian figure of Voss. He is more intent and successful than any harshness of geography or disease in searching out the weaknesses of his companions. In a situation in which life itself depends upon the naked force of will, he is seen, terrifyingly, to concentrate in himself an essential part of everyone else's humanity. Everyone's will is fused into Voss's. The question posed is whether any human situation can be just the realisation of a pure abstraction like the will. Each member of the party clings to something else, to some other standard supplied by a different life – the young Frank Le Mesurier to his poetry, Judd the ex-convict to the common kindness of a family man, Palfreyman to his science and his religion, Turner and Angus to a protective selfishness. But all in the end are consumed by the violence of Voss's burning will. 'By some process of chemical choice, the cavalcade had resolved itself into immutable component parts. No one denied that Mr Voss was the first, the burning element, that consumed obstacles, as well as indifference in others' (p. 258). The Aborigines are the one form of humanity which evades the absoluteness of Voss's control. Their existence is purely a passage from moment to moment, hardly directed at all by the conscious will. They drift as easily as smoke and are as responsive to the play of the physical life about them. They cannot in fact be positively separated from it, they never take on sufficient antagonist force for Voss to meet and overcome. It is 'right', in keeping with the nature of the fiction itself, that it should be these, surviving as they do by the negation of active will, who in the horrifying end, when the party has split into two fragments, destroy Voss.

If the first narrative line has to do with the world of 'semblance' or reality, the physical progress of the expedition itself, the second has to do with the world of 'dream' and the life of the spirit; and this as it is focused in the relationship of Voss and Laura. (Not that the Voss–Laura relationship is the sole subject-matter: there is also much sharp, and comic, social observation of the colonial scene.) The only physical substratum for the relationship is the few brief meetings of Voss and Laura before the expedition leaves. On this the imagination of each, moved by deep emotional hunger, constructs a pattern of feeling of great richness, delicacy and conviction. The fact that the relationship evolves by means of an intense and reciprocal empathy causes the reader no incredulity or discomfort because he senses an essential propriety between the nature of the experience and its poetic treatment. If a writer has the creative strength, the sincerity and the tact in realisation which Patrick White shows himself abundantly to possess, he can, and the reader accepts that he can, allow himself a considerable degree of freedom from the logic of a straight-forward representational method. The relationship of Voss and Laura, then, progresses from its simple beginning by means of a sympathetic parallelism into a 'fearful symmetry'. I use the famous phrase advisedly to suggest that blend of love, terror and harmony which the relationship achieves in the moments before Voss and Laura are finally destroyed, he by the journey, she, in resonance, by a total collapse of mind and body.

The novel concludes quietly in the third section in a muted repetition and reminiscence of the positive vision – never too firmly or abstractly formulated – generated by the substance of the novel. Patrick White uses the psychology of the explorer as a metaphor of man. The explorer lives at extremes, on borders and edges; he is always pushing back the frontiers of suffering, and suffering is the universal experience of extremity uniting man. Voss is the purest example of the explorer's psychology, but he is saved from unconvincing super-humanity by a grubby stain of backsliding man. There is a touch of malignancy, of Hitler, in the way he treats his companions. This, paradoxically, makes his illumination – conversion is too revivalist a word – which is religious in its source and derived from the acceptance which is part of his love for Laura, possible, and when it takes place, convincing. Only the sinful man can become the redeemed man. *Voss* embodies the belief, or rather perception, of the novelist that simplicity and suffering are the conditions for the re-making of man. The suffering is sustained and terrible; the simplicity only barely and painfully achieved at the point of dissolution.

There are many fine things in the novel which if not quite at, must certainly be near, the top of White's achievement. Among them are the treatment of the religious theme, the deployment of the historical sense, the perception of Australian experience, the varied use of the novelist's language. Perhaps I could look at each of these for a moment.

An unpretentious account of the spiritual theme in *Voss* is given by G. A. Wilkes in his *Australian Literature: A Conspectus*:

> Voss leads an expedition across the Australian continent in order to mortify and exalt himself by suffering, as though in rivalry with Christ, to prove that man may become God. . .Voss seeks transcendence through a supreme egotism. What makes him so compelling a figure, however, is rather his vulnerability in this attempt. He must try to extinguish all human feeling in himself, not only by welcoming the privations of the journey, but also by repelling all emotions of fellowship – the suspicion that he

may be thought to love his dog, Gyp, compels him to execute her forthwith.[4]

This plain statement has much to recommend it in its temperance and straightforwardness. It is developed in a more metaphysical way in an impressive essay, 'The Gothic Splendours', by the distinguished Australian poet James McAuley. He shows that *Voss* aims to produce effects more commonly found or attempted in poetry. He even suggests that *Voss* fulfils this aim with greater depth and more sustained intensity than most Australian poetry. McAuley sees *Voss* as a story organised around the contrast between the urban society of Sydney and the unexplored Bush: provincial gentility, commercialism, conventional piety, on the one side; on the other, the world of extremes in which concealment and compromises are torn away. Not that *Voss* relies on this too-simple contrast. The world of Sydney, for example, *is* the Bush, 'the country of the mind' (p. 475), for Laura. The Bush pictures an inner world that the urban man may enter also 'if he has the courage and metaphysical depth to explore his selfhood and his relation to God'.[5] The conquest of a continent is the outward aspect of Voss's inward expedition. 'What Voss is dedicated to is the self-deification of man, to be achieved in his own person, through boundless will and pride and daring.'[6] To be self-subsistent, self-sufficient, God requires one to abhor humility and to need no one.

According to McAuley, White's novel is not simply the realisation of a purely fantastic eccentric theme, the megalomania of an individual, but the use of this view to interpret imaginatively a tension within modern civilisation. McAuley's reservation about *Voss* has to do with the 'wary evasiveness' with which this issue is finally handled. 'The Christian framework is assumed in the book for the purpose of stating the issues, and up to a point for resolving them. But in the last part the framework of interpretation seems itself to slip and become unclear.'[7] McAuley's essay, which is one of the best accounts of the religious and metaphysical reading of *Voss*, finally blames Patrick White, it appears, for using the Christian framework instead of believing it. But this seems to me to misunderstand the nature of the artist's possibly unscrupulous use of whatever lies to hand in the way of means for helping him to realise his perception. I see nothing improper in White's use of the Christian myth. The only question is whether it is successful, whether his use of it is adequate for his artistic purpose. I have no doubt it is adequate and that it is used successfully.

Not that the treatment is without flaw. Here is a passage from the latter part of the book in which Laura, now a respected headmistress as well as a still suffering woman, is talking to Judd, now a worn and ancient man, who is the sole survivor of Voss's expedition.

> 'You know, Judd, Miss Trevelyan was a friend of Mr Voss.'
>
> 'Ah,' smiled the aged, gummy man, 'Voss.'
>
> He looked at the ground, but presently spoke again.
>
> 'Voss left his mark on the country,' he said.
>
> 'How?' asked Miss Trevelyan, cautiously.
>
> 'Well, the trees, of course. He was cutting his initials in the trees. He was a queer beggar, Voss. The blacks talk about him to this day. He is still there – that is the honest opinion of many of them – he is there in the country, and always will be.'. . .
>
> 'He was more than a man.' Judd continued, with the gratified air of one who had found that for which he had been looking. 'He was a Christian, such as I understand it.'
>
> Miss Trevelyan was holding a handkerchief to her lips, as though her life-blood might gush out.
>
> 'Not according to my interpretation of the word,' the Colonel interrupted, remorselessly, 'not by what I have heard.'
>
> 'Poor fellow,' sighed old Sanderson, again unhappy. 'He was somewhat twisted. But he is dead and gone.'
>
> Now that he was launched, Judd was determined to pursue his wavering way.
>
> 'He would wash the sores of the men. He would sit all night with them when they were sick, and clean up their filth with his own hands. I cried, I tell you, after he was dead. There was none of us could believe it when we saw the spear, hanging from his side, and shaking.' (pp. 472–3)

This passage shows both the strength and weakness of White's method. On the one hand, we have the living presentation of a scene, the indirect glimpses of Voss which credibilise his character while underlining his strangeness, the characteristically shrewd collocation of varied characters, and the rapid, progressive movement of the narrative. On the other hand, we have what is admittedly poor doddering Judd's jumbled memory, the product of a disordered mind, age, and the guilt of his desertion, but the last paragraph still appears as a theatrical parallel. Judd's vision of Voss's death with the spear quivering in his side spoils, with its extraneous, geometric symbolism, the crispness and effectiveness of this part of the novel, and shows itself as something arranged and imported.

I have referred already to the imaginative authenticity produced in the first part of the novel by Patrick White's sensitive historical feeling, the strange blend of the Pacific and the Victorian, of colonial blandness and commercial values, and their convincing realisation in the Bonner household and its connections. And Voss himself, as R. F. Brissenden points out, belongs very closely to that group of historical characters 'particularly artists, intellectuals or explorers (and Voss is all three), [who] seem, more often than not, to have seen their actions either in a religious light or in a light conditioned by the absence of religion'.[8] The imaginative truth with which Voss is grasped, is matched with the skill in which the tone and manners of both the middle-class and the upper-class of colonial society in nineteenth-century Sydney are evoked. This second observation can be tested in the third part of the novel in which the ethos, assumptions and response of the superior people of the time are beautifully felt and lucidly explicated. The thin snobberies of the Misses Linleys' Academy for Young Ladies, where Laura Trevelyan was first a resident mistress then the headmistress; the self-assured glitter of Colonel Hebden and Mrs de Courcey; the combination of show and vigour in the great Sydney parties of the time – all these are exhibited with an infallible social acumen and an unerring ear for idiom.

The third fine thing in *Voss*, as I noted earlier, is the perception of Australian experience. In the final section we see Voss moving from the present into the historical and then into myth. Voss, and a central truth about, or experience of, Australia itself have become one. Australia is almost another character in the novel, certainly an impressive and influential force, the complex presence of which affects the organisation and the feeling of the novel at many different points. Australia is the sole opponent worthy of Voss's will. The will to know Australia is the initiating impulse of the novel. It is Australia which appears in Laura's letters to Voss as the necessary and mysterious context and passion of Voss himself; and to know him requires her to experience the land. To experience here means not only, or not just, external or physical acquaintance. Rather, it is the mode of knowledge possessed by Jackie, the Aborigine who becomes a legend among the tribes:

> He became a legend amongst the tribes. Of the great country through which he travelled constantly, he was the shifting and troubled mind. His voice would issue out of his lungs, and wrestle with the rocks, until it was thrown back at him. He was always speaking with the souls of those who had died in the land, and was ready to translate their wishes into dialect. (pp. 448–9)

Or as Laura says herself, at the end of a novel powerfully charged with the experience, the colour, and the significance of Australia itself:

> 'I am uncomfortably aware of the very little I have seen and experienced of things in general, and of our country in particular. . .but the little I have seen is less, I like to feel, than what I know. Knowledge was never a matter of geography. Quite the reverse, it overflows all maps that exist. Perhaps true knowledge only comes of death by torture in the country of the mind.' (p. 475)

If the novel communicates the human significance of the Australian continent, if the expedition is an apt metaphor for the stresses of human life, if Voss himself becomes a lucent symbol of man and his struggle, this is because the country and the landscape are evoked with precision and solidity, and because Voss's complex, flawed and stricken humanity is rendered with marvellous actuality and fullness. He can be, in Henry James's phrase, in the preface to *What Maisie Knew*, 'the striking figured symbol' because he is 'the thoroughly pictured creature'. Eyre's *Journal* supplies White for *Voss*, as Shelvoake's *Voyages* supplied

Coleridge for *The Ancient Mariner*, a work treating a similar theme with a period, a system of assumption, a protagonist, a drama and a context which powerfully attracted the author's profoundest feelings and unloosed that flow of unconscious forces of which Coleridge wrote in *On Poesy or Art*:

> In every work of art there is a reconcilement of the external and the internal, the conscious is so impressed on the unconscious as to appear in it. . .He who combines the two is the man of genius; and for that reason he must partake of both. Hence there is in genius itself an unconscious activity: nay, that is the genius in the man of genius.

White in *Voss* displays the faculty Coleridge meant by genius here, and in addition he shows those gifts of management and discriminating skill which enable him to embody and make visible his perceptions.

Finally, I chose the novelist's use of language as one of the most impressive qualities of this novel. It is marked by a most notable and positive force, which suggests an artist struggling ferociously with words in order to bend them to his purposes. In the pursuit of this, White allows himself great freedom in respect of many of the informalities of English, wrenching the syntax and pushing the language to its limits. It is a use of language which issues naturally into metaphor, sometimes into jostling clusters of it. It is accompanied, too, by a certain quality of opacity which yields on most occasions to reflection but which requires of the reader an energy of thought and response corresponding to what the writer has put into it. White's use of language is wholly different from that which provoked Coleridge to ask in *Anima Poetae* (1802):

> *Quaere*, whether or no too great definiteness of terms in any language may not consume to much of the vital and idea-creating force in distinct, clear, full-made images, and so prevent originality. For original might be distinguished from positive thought.

White never consumes the vital force in pursuit of utter clarity. But as soon as one has said this, his skill with a different kind of idiom has also to be noted, for example in the third part of the novel where it is most appropriate, where he uses speech

remarkable for its elegance and urbanity. Barry Argyle noted[9]
how White chose two styles to convey the differences of intention
and circumstances of Sydney society on the one hand, and of
the members of the expedition on the other: the first less poetic,
less self-revealing and more apt for ironic deception; the second
a language packed with metaphor and projecting the obsessed
and fanatic nature of Voss. Here, as an illustration of what I
have been saying, is the opening page of the novel, in which
the theme of exploration is matched with a technique which is
itself poetic and exploratory:

> 'There is a man here, miss, asking for your uncle,'
> said Rose.
> And stood breathing.
> 'What man?' asked the young woman, who was
> engaged upon some embroidery of a difficult nature, at
> which she was now forced to look more closely, holding
> a little frame to the light. 'Or is it perhaps a gentleman?'
> 'I do not know,' said the servant. 'It is a kind of foreign
> man.'
> Something had made this woman monotonous. Her big
> breasts moved dully as she spoke, or she would stand, and
> the weight of her silences impressed itself on strangers. If
> the more sensitive amongst those she served or addressed
> failed to look at Rose, it was because her manner seemed
> to accuse the conscience, or it could have been, more simply,
> that they were embarrassed by her harelip.
> 'A foreigner?' said her mistress, and her Sunday dress
> signed. 'It can only be the German.'
> It was now the young woman's duty to give some order.
> In the end she would perform that duty with authority and
> distinction, but she did always hesitate at first. She would
> seldom have come out of herself for choice, for she was
> happiest shut with her own thoughts, and such was the
> texture of her marble, few people ever guessed at these.
> (p. 9)

We catch the unmistakable White manner: the beginning without
preliminaries, the intense seriousness of attitude, and the effort
to describe experience in such a way that the account partakes
itself in what it is referring to. We see the dislocation of syntax,

the naturally figured narrative, and the employment of modes one tends to think of as more at home in poetry. That lopsided 'And stood breathing' conveys the anxiety and the heaviness of Rose's personality, just as her engagement upon 'embroidery of a difficult nature' and 'the texture of her marble' communicate the coolness and the fineness of Laura's. The language itself is an instrument which establishes in a palpable, solid way both the character and the meaning of Voss, a man who is to be above all outside and beyond the ordinary run of mankind.

Even by Patrick White's standards, *Riders in the Chariot* is a novel remarkable for its richness of content, and it adds to this a more conscious rigour of pattern. If the form disclosed by *Voss* is that of a route or path, the design of *Riders in the Chariot* suggests a knot. The lives of four people, utterly different in character and provenance, are tied together in the mean suburb of Sarsaparilla. Their differences are marvellously realised. The lives of the crazy Miss Hare, Himmelfarb the survivor of the Nazi camps, Mrs Godbold the East Anglian immigrant, and Dubbo the tubercular painter, are unfolded with the utmost assurance and the most inward conviction. Miss Hare, a misshapen example of the decaying gentry, is related to Theodora Goodman; Mrs Godbold, the unpretentious working woman, to Julia Fallon in *The Living and the Dead*; and Dubbo the half-caste painter looks forward, at least in part of his nature, to Hurtle Duffield in *The Vivisector*. But the most fully developed, the most original and powerful creation in the work, is Himmelfarb, the history and reality of whose Jewish experience are evoked with the most solid and accurate understanding. The scope of the work is extraordinary and the control light and unstrained.

The group is united by their possession of a secret gift, the immediate apprehension of reality and values by modes of understanding neglected or despised by the common run of men. I am reminded again of some of the phrases I quoted earlier (p. 29) from Lawrence's letter about the old Viennese lady: '. . .only the other world of pure being matters. . .the just sense of values. . .She has. . .taken her place in the realities. . .she *knows* what life consists of. . .'. This taking of a place among the realities, this knowledge of what life consists in, and this never failing that knowledge, make up the faculty or organ of consciousness which, while independent of experience, makes itself felt gradually through the articulation of the characters' lives. The chariot, biblical and Blakean, is the symbol of this consciousness. The concept of the chariot comes to Himmelfarb during his studies of ancient Rabbinical mystical works, and is cloudily gathered by Miss Hare by means of an almost non-human instinct for the otherness of the natural world of plants and animals. It appears to each, to Himmelfarb, to Miss Hare, and to Dubbo and Mrs Godbold, in an idiom appropriate to his or her nature. At one point Himmelfarb relates it to Jewish spirituality:

> 'That, I am not sure,' he replied. 'It is difficult to distinguish. Just when I think I have understood, I discover some fresh form – so many – streaming with implications. There is the Throne of God, for instance. That is obvious enough – all gold, and chrysoprase, and jasper. Then there is the Chariot of Redemption, much more shadowy, poignant, personal. And the faces of the riders. I cannot begin to see the expression of the faces.' (p. 151)

Forms streaming with implication: the phrase carries with it an intimation of the nature of this special non-discursive apprehension which the world of substance fails to recognise or fears. It is a sense of pure being, of the radiance of existence. It is a gift of which suffering is the necessary condition and the recognition of which in others depends upon one's possession of it. It invariably provokes persecution. It is because the gift has to do with the clarity of existence that it provokes evil in those who are committed to negation. The evil may be bland as in Mrs Jolley, the persecutor of Miss Hare, or chummy as in the workmates who ravage Himmelfarb in a mock crucifixion, or monstrously abstract as in the Germany of the ovens, where 'the guards might laugh at some indignity glimpsed, but on the whole, at the assembly point, they seemed to prefer a darkness in which to hate in the abstract the whole mass of Jews' (p. 192). Evil does always contain this note of vacancy, of shadowy non-being. The conflict between the enlightened and the rest is not simply, therefore, one of human antagonism but is something raised to a metaphysical and religious plane.

I hope I have not here given any impression that the idea has escaped from the fiction into some parabolic or mystically symbolic world. That would be the opposite of the truth. One is in fact sunk deeply into the other, and the novel is a striking manifestation of the true novelist's specification of Keats's negative capability, which is, paradoxically, the positive power effortlessly to enter into other lives and other experiences and with equal authority and ease project them into language and images which have for the reader both the validity of the original experience and the accessibility of its new state. One small but significant example of this gift of White is his concern with *things*. Throughout this novel the nuclear life of objects has an extraordinary importance and is conveyed with a poet's power. Objects help to make palpable the most fleeting of metaphysical experiences, and they give weight and solidity to a narrative concerned with what is mysterious and difficult. White in much of his work attempts to convey the inward life of objects and sometimes, particularly in the case of scenery, this tricks him into an exaggerated use of the pathetic fallacy. But in *Riders in the Chariot* the intrinsic vitality of objects has as part of its being its meaning for the handler and observer. The centre of Miss Hare's character depends upon her effort empathically to become, not merely to grasp, the nature and existence of what she encounters in the non-human world. This is true whether in her moods of despair:

> Later, when she got up from the ground, she did not attempt to inquire into what might have bludgeoned her numb mind and aching body, for night had come, cold and black. She bruised knuckle on knuckle, to try to stop her shivering, and began to feel her way through the house, by stages of brocade, and vicious gilt, by slippery tortoiseshell and coldest, unresponsive marble. (p. 41)

Or in her moods of rapture:

> Although no other human being was actually present, she did resent what must eventually recur. She stroked leaves sulkily. She broke a shaggy stick. Other people would drive along a bush road looking out of the windows of a car, but their minds embraced almost nothing of what their

flickering eyes saw. Whole towers of green remained unclimbed, rocks unopened. Or else the intruders might stop their cars, and go in search of water. She had seen them, letting themselves down into the cold, black, secret rock pools, while remaining enclosed in their own resentful gooseflesh. Whereas she, Miss Hare, whose eyes were always probing, fingers trying, would achieve the ecstasy of complete, annihilating liberation without any such immersion. (p. 12)

Objects are also used in the more external and traditionally professional way to evoke a personality and define its bias. Mordecai Himmelfarb's father, Moshe, for example, is a worldly Jew of liberal tastes who believes that the age of enlightenment and universal brotherhood had dawned in Western Europe and who loved to give expensive presents and cultivate the Gentiles:

Mordecai remembered the silk hats in which his father presented himself, on civic and religious occasions alike. Ordered from an English hatter, Moshe's hats reflected that nice perfection which may be attained by the reasonable man. For Moshe Himmelfarb was nothing less. If he was also nothing more, that was after other, exacting, not to say reactionary standards, by which such lustrous hats could only be judged vain, hollow and lamentably fragile.' (p. 109)

That this weak and amiable man should be converted to Christianity, as to a new fashion, and marry a young Gentile after his wife's death, is something that one would expect not just from his character but from his hat.

Moshe Himmelfarb is but one of a host of minor characters jostling on every page and compelling, in their vitality, the reader's attention at every point. There is, for instance, the muted seriousness of Mordecai's wife Reha; there is that other renegade Jew, an appealing Judas, Mr Rosetree who runs the factory where Himmelfarb works in Australia, and where Dubbo, as a general handyman, sweeps the floors; there are the menacingly bland housekeeper Mrs Jolley and her repulsively 'nice' croney Mrs Flack; there is the delinquent Blue, the corrupting clergyman Mr Calderon, and Mr Theobalds the factory foreman who, when Himmelfarb is jocularly 'crucified' by his workmates, helps him down from the cross with a comforting explanation of the Australian theory of social play:

'Remember,' Ernie Theobalds continued, 'We have a sense of humour, and when the boys start to horse around, it is that that is gettin' the better of 'em. They can't resist a joke. Even when a man is full of beer, you will find the old sense of humour hard at work underneath. It has to play a joke. See? No offence can be taken where a joke is intended.' (p. 468)

But for all their spilling and prodigal life, none of these distract the reader from the main line or blur its pattern. The four main lives through which the author's vision is transmitted (and vision is an appropriate term because White is engaged here with a force which, to quote some words from *Voss*, causes the 'world of substance to quake') are shown with that creative authenticity derived from the marriage of absolute fidelity of observation to imaginative power. The tubercular half-caste is someone in whom one sees an essential flavour of Australia, and Dubbo's grasp of reality through the concreteness of painting is something White feels a peculiar personal sympathy for and an astonishing power to communicate. Miss Hare once more embodies that extraordinary, Lawrentian feeling for other than human forms of life which, as we see in Lawrence, can educate into the highest wisdom, and her tainted genealogy is something that White again shows an intimacy of understanding for. Mrs Godbold represents, as does Stan Parker, simplicity, normality, the central traditional morality raised by gentleness and candour to the point of genius. And this, too, is a nature highly attractive to White which he has dealt with on more than one occasion. Himmelfarb, the central figure of the book, is a wholly new creation, European, Jewish, learned, saintly. Not only he but the cultivated middle-class German-Jewish tradition to which he belongs, its context and character, its strength and weakness, are conveyed with extraordinary inwardness and force and without a single false touch or distortion. How splendidly and accurately we feel the ritual and discipline of Hebrew practice and its combination of a strong tribal and family quality with the pure, remote spirit of Jewish religion, or of religion itself.

Himmelfarb's enlightenment, as we see with Voss, is not

something which he has earned by effort, nor is it the simple progression and maturing of his inheritance. It is a gift, a grace. It has survived his own doubt, sensuality, infidelity, boredom, treachery and the persecution of others, but its residue in Himmelfarb is a total clarity of understanding which enables him, like Lawrence's old Madame Stepniak, to take his place in the realities and to know what life consists in and never to fail in that knowledge.

Patrick White is a writer who habitually sees experience as cast into polarities. Sometimes these are of an almost Manichaean violence. In the present novel there is a central opposition between the enlightened consciousness, in its various forms, and conventional modes of thought. A second tension works through the novel. Himmelfarb puts it like this in a conversation with his wife's practical, eldest brother whom he finds in Israel after his escape from Germany, although escape is too active a way to describe the series of steps and accidents which brings him passively for the briefest visit to the land: 'I would only point out that spiritual faith is also an active force. Which will populate the world after each attempt by the men of action to destroy it' (p. 214). But as well as the opposition of faith and action, there is also that between the individual and the community. In much of White, the community shows itself as savage and dangerous and destructive of individuality. The antagonism may be gross as in Nazi Germany or rough and mocking as in the Australian factory. It can be uncomprehending and uneasy as among Himmelfarb's co-religionists or guilty and uncomprehending as among the liberal Germans. But the conflict between enlightened consciousness and the habitual understanding of sensible men, as between faith and action, constantly works itself out in the persecution of the individual by the group. Clarity of understanding, and the acceptance of the purity of being, are things which men in society find disruptive of their bonds and conventions. Society, in fact, is the inveterate enemy of the spiritual life.

R. F. Brissenden in a sensitive treatment of White's work takes exception to White's implied equation of Nazi evil and Australian uncouthness:

It is patently White's intention to suggest, through

Himmelfarb's 'crucifixion', that within an ordinary suburb the same evil forces which animated Nazi Germany exist, at least potentially. The intention, unfortunately, is not completely realised. One reason may be that societies just do differ qualitatively: the hell of Auschwitz and Buchenwald is not the hell of Australian suburbia, and to equate them must inevitably seem grotesquely disproportionate. Ordinary people may behave monstrously, but only under extraordinary pressures, and these do not at present appear to operate in Australia. Such communal cruelty as does occur is usually the cruelty of neglect, ignorance or an amused and shallow contempt.[10]

One can appreciate the indignation which rejects the roughness of Australian factory workers as being in any way the counterpart of Nazi evil. On the other hand, it seems to me that this is to take a sociological view of White's undertaking. He is not concerned, surely, with the relative merits of two societies but with the indissoluble connection of forms of human evil. Each, whether extreme or near, comes from the corrupt will or the clouded understanding. Each in its way is a mode of non-being.

Just as the grades of evil are connected, so there is a unity supporting 'the rungs of faith' or the ladder of goodness. Just as the party of evil can stretch from the Nazis to the factory workers, so that of good includes in its membership the sanctity of Himmelfarb, the crazed integrity of Miss Hare, the aloof disinterestedness of Dubbo and the folk goodness of Mrs Godbold. Indeed, these four, drawn from the ends of the earth and brought together in this remote and unlikely place, correspond to, or indeed are, the hidden *zaddikim*.

> 'In each generation,' [says Himmelfarb to Miss Hare] 'we say, there are thirty-six hidden *zaddikim* – holy men who go secretly about the world, healing, interpreting, doing their good deeds.'. . .
> 'It is even told. . .how the creative light of God poured into the *zaddikim*. That *they* are the Chariot of God.' (p. 173)

In fact, we see here how the technique of the novel, the skilful sewing by which these utterly disparate lives are brought

together, is exquisitely in symmetry with the central theme of
the novel – the existence of a party of goodness and being, and
the singular and profound and secret unity which binds its
members together. This, in fact, is the highest kind of technique,
the best answer to Leavis's question: 'Is there any great novelist
whose preoccupation with "form" is not a matter of his
responsibility towards a rich human interest, or complexity of
interests, profoundly realised? – a responsibility involving, of its
nature, imaginative sympathy, moral discrimination and
judgement of relative human value?'[11]

Having made this large but, I believe, fully warranted claim
for Patrick White, I feel obliged at once to point to certain
nagging deficiencies in this novel. Pure and reverent and
appropriate as is the author's attitude to the *zaddikim*, the four
beautifully realised heroes of the novel, the one he displays to
others in the novel, and particularly to the workers in the factory
and the ordinary people in the suburb, is disproportionately
contemptuous. There is something pinched and negative in the
tone and idiom he uses, for example, about the workers in Mr
Rosetree's Brighta Bicycle Lamps factory:

> Ladies sat at their assembly trays, and repeated with dainty
> skill the single act they would be called on to perform. Or
> eased their plastic teeth. Or shifted gum. . .And gentlemen
> in singlets, who stood with their hands on their hips, or
> rolled limp-looking cigarettes, or consulted the sporting
> page, and even, when it was absolutely necessary, con-
> descended to lean forward and take part in some mechanical
> ritual which still demanded their presence. (p. 223)

> So the plastic ladies and the pursy men bent their heads
> above their benches. Toothless lads hawked up a mirthless
> laughter, while the faces of the girls let it be understood
> that nobody would take advantage of them. (p. 229)

The feeling here is not so much indignation as disgust – the lips
seem to writhe at the 'ladies' and 'gentlemen' – and not so much
deserved as self-indulgently released. In the second place, the
dislocations of syntax which White can use, for example at the
beginning of *Voss*, with the most effective originality, sometimes,
particularly in these disdainful scenes, become nearly mechanical.

For example, it seems pointless to use so portentous an idiom
to describe the movements of a typist in Mr Rosetree's office:

> 'If you will pass this way,' almost shouted the plump
> goddess, perspiring on her foam rubber.
> She feared the situation was making her conspicuous.
> 'Thank you,' Himmelfarb replied, and smiled at the
> hand which indicated doors.
> She did not rise, of course, having reduced her obli-
> gations at the salary received. But let her hand fall.
> (p. 224)

There is a certain dimming of critical alertness at these points,
which seems to betray too personal an engagement of the author
with the material in hand and too little control of his personal
impulses. A similar failure of taste occurs at one of the climaxes
of the novel when Himmelfarb is tied to a cross in a rough parody
of the Crucifixion by his workmates in the factory. The actual
episode is described with a sort of tittering burlesque and made
to fit exactly into a context of hearty Australian matiness and
philistine cruelty. But while there could be no questioning the
propriety of White's use of the Crucifixion story, he cannot resist
the temptation to make the analogy too complete. One worker
holds up a cloth to the crucified Himmelfarb's lips; Miss Hare
sees the marble shudder and crack in her great, run-down house,
Xanadu; Himmelfarb is taken down from the cross into the arms
of Mrs Godbold, one of the faithful women; and poor Mr
Rosetree, the renegade Jew, an appealing Judas, commits suicide
in his bathroom. Nothing is wanting to complete the reflection
of Calvary.

Patrick White belongs to a line of novelists whose art
embodies a concentrated and dazzling vision of man. Such writers
are not manipulators of plot, or cultivators of a sensibility, or
critics of manners, or chroniclers of a period. Their art is initiated
by their vision and its form is determined more by a force from
within than by an extrinsic scaffolding. These writers are not
lacking in the capacity for the most inclusive and most significant
kind of design. And while in some work of this nature minute
particulars tend to melt away in the glow of vision, this is
certainly not so with Patrick White, in whose novels the multiple
detail is perpetually sharp and fresh. It is somewhere between

imaginative power, and authenticity and crispness of detail that Patrick White's work is imperfect, in the area where architectural capacity and taste are required. The failure is not in the generating concept nor in the worked-out detail – neither in the idea nor the vocabulary, that is – but somewhere between in what one might call the syntactical structure. *Voss* and *Riders in the Chariot* certainly answer this account, I believe: impressive in the constructive idea, superb in their palpable concreteness, weaker in the passages of transition and apt on occasion to offer neatness and gratuitous accretion in place of organic design. This is the other, feebler side of Patrick White's massive integrity of vision.

It is this more generous and powerful part of White's sensibility which finds expression in the second part of the novel. The beam of attention passes across this almost heraldic design to fasten on the other two members of the *zaddikim*, Mrs Godbold and Dubbo, the painter. Mrs Godbold, an East-Anglian immigrant, whose father was a cobbler with a devotion to duty, draws her solid and luminous innocence from the fen life and country which White indicates with exact and delicate appreciation.

> In the flat, fen country from which she had come, she grew to expect what is called monotony by those who are deaf to the variations on it. A grey country. Even though a hollyhock in her father's garden would sometimes flicker up in memory against a grey wall, or rose straggle over eaves, or bosomy elm heave in the heavy summer, it was winter that she remembered best, of many, many greys: boots clattering through grey streets; the mirror-grey of winter fens; naked elms tossing rooks into a mackerel sky; the cathedral – the greyest, the most permanent of all greys, rising into cloud, that sometimes would disperse, sometimes would unite with stone. (p. 262)

Her husband, imprisoned in his brutishness, concentrates on beer, sex and the trots. Mrs Godbold is living in a shed at Sarsaparilla where she bears children and takes in washing, but Mrs Godbold, both in her pitiful squalor here and in the home of the Chalmers-Robinsons where she had been a maid, was always capable of experiences that can only be described as mystical:

Alone in the house – for the cook would retire into livery indolence, and the gardener had a down on somebody, and the chauffeur was almost never there, for driving the mistress about the town – the maid would attempt to express her belief, not in words, nor in the attitudes of orthodox worship, but in the surrender of herself to a state of passive adoration, in which she would allow her substantial body to dissolve into a loveliness of air and light, magnolia scent, and dove psalmody. Or, in the performance of her duties, polishing plate, scrubbing floors, mending the abandoned stockings, gathering the slithery dresses from where they had fallen, searching carpets for silverfish, and furs for moth, she could have been offering up the active essence of her being in unstinted praise. And had some left over for a further expression of faith to which she had not been led. Whenever the door-bell rang, she would search the faces of strangers to discover whether she would be required to testify. Always it seemed that some of her strength would be left over to give, for, willing though she was to sacrifice herself in any way to her mistress, the latter would never emerge from her own distraction to receive. (p. 275)

Her utterly convincing integrity, shown at its most exquisite during the horrifying scene of soiled and gritty corruption at Mrs Khalil's home brothel, where Mrs Godbold goes to collect her husband, is but one example of White's extraordinary inwardness of empathy with women, which for intensity and range can hardly be equalled in modern fiction.

In the present novel, for example, not only do we have Miss Hare and Mrs Godbold, totally different specifications of the extraordinary woman, but we have in addition a variety of quickly but thoroughly realised minor women: the sinister Mrs Jolley and Mrs Flack, the neurotic Mrs Chalmers-Robinson, Mrs Godbold's typist daughter Hannah, the prostitute Else, and Mrs Shirl Rosetree, who could so convince herself of her non-Jewish character, that after going softly into the kitchen to heat up some chicken soup with Mrs Kneidlach and to taste the chopped chicken livers she had bullied her daily into making, she could ask of her suffering husband, 'What can you expect of Jews?' (p. 494). Each of these minor characters has the stamp of coherence but also includes that 'savour of discrepancy', of individual oddity, that Henry James welcomed as a signal of life. The women in this novel are, of course, human before they are women – if one can use the word 'before' in a metaphorical way – and they both stand for and oppose reality or are indifferent to it or evade it. What White succeeds in doing is to convey the essential human quality of a whole range of female persons with the subtlest imaginative sympathy, and in a way that gives body and resonance both to the theme of his novel and to its quality as a composition.

Range or reach, the strength of distance, is evident also in the introduction, in the latter part of the novel, of Alf Dubbo, a bright boy of mixed race who was reared in a small town among black gins dressed in cast-off clothing waiting to be picked up by white youths and older drunks. He was taken in by the Anglican rector, Timothy Calderon and his sister Mrs Pask, in pursuit of their high ideals in a process they called their Great Experiment. He was educated by Mr Calderon, taught painting by Mrs Pask, seduced by the homosexual rector, and dismissed by his sister. His life after that was spent wandering through, and living off, the country, consorting with ageing drabs, hanging about country towns and stations, but never staying anywhere long since he might be arrested for a crime or confined to a reserve. His body was riddled with sickness, venereal and tubercular, but his life was spent pursuing his vocation, which enabled him 'to ignore for the most part what people called life'. Dubbo is at the furthest extreme in Australian life from the gentility of Miss Hare or the inner tranquillity of Mrs Godbold or the learning and sanctity of Himmelfarb. But he shares with each of them his vision and he is as devoted to it as they. For Dubbo, pure being, reality, just values, are to be approached through the intensity and rhythm of painting and supremely through the effort to paint his vision of *The Chariot*. He ends up as a floor sweeper in the factory where Himmelfarb works and he senses in Himmelfarb his membership of the community.

White has a rare faculty for communicating the almost muscular struggle of the painter to achieve his vision, his effort to carve from solid paint the content of his insight. Above all he succeeds in conveying the validity of Dubbo's vocation and the proximity it gives him to purity of being and utter singleness of purpose. All the illuminated, the four members of the *zaddikim*, fail, their lives are completed by ruin. Dubbo dies of a tubercular haemorrhage, Miss Hare's great house, Xanadu, is razed to make way for suburbia, Himmelfarb after his 'crucifixion' dies in Mrs Godbold's care, Mrs Godbold goes mildly on seeming 'to live for irrelevance', developing 'a love and respect for common objects and trivial acts' (p. 536). But this, one grasps, is simply the condition and the fulfilment of their existence, has no relevance to the value of their lives or what they stand for. In each of these, this extraordinary novel confirms, there is achieved the success the world hates and needs.

In the third section of *Voss* there occur some lines – I have referred to them before – which are an apt epigraph for *Riders in the Chariot*: 'It was his niece, Laura Trevelyan, who had caused Mr Bonner's world of substance to quake' (p. 373). Causing the world of substance to quake is the great shaping activity working through *Riders in the Chariot*. The world of substance exposed in the novel includes not only the hard, thick, resistant one of common life and convention but other and odder worlds too: the world of a crazy specimen of the decayed Australian gentry, the world of an unpretentious working woman, the world of a persecuted German Jew, the world of an uprooted Aborigine. In addition, each of the characters in which these worlds are defined and examined gives access to one species of a fourfold variety of experience: experience of the natural world, of plants and animals through Miss Hare's nearly non-human instinct for otherness, of family virtue and neighbourliness in Mrs Godbold, of sanctity in Himmelfarb, and of art in the painting of Dubbo. The four lives, the separate worlds, different orders of experience, connect, in a skilfully managed and natural way, in Sarsaparilla. But perhaps, one feels, on reflection, what I referred to at the beginning as a more conscious design, and later as a composition, and just now as skilful management, includes just a degree too much deliberation, a shade too much calculation in the arrangement. After all, as John Updike wrote, 'What we want from our great imaginers is not fuel but fire, not patterns but an action, not fragmented and interlaced accounts but a story.'[12] The story of manifold voice is powerful, cogent, human. But perhaps the framework is still a touch too external, the design too clearly articulated, too deliberately managed.

4 Other Work

The scope of the eleven stories in *The Burnt Ones* (1964) is naturally more confined than in the novels, but the shape and proportions are the same. There is a similar sense of the depth of human nature and the same strikingly individual sensibility, giving off a mixed odour of sweat and spirituality. The people in the Australian group of stories may be ordinary ('Dead Roses', 'Willy-Wagtails by Moonlight') or drab ('Clay', 'Down at the Dump'), the events few and unspectacular, the context conventional or down at heel, the air wretched or melancholy, and yet from these unpromising constituents Patrick White constructs a celebration of human possibility which is at once lyrical and quite unsentimental. White has an eye which is gluttonous for detail. Each passage is firm from the presence of discriminated actuality. But all the solid, objective existence, convincing in surface, sure in implication, is submissive to the initiative of the writer. It is as much the result of reflection as observation, and it is composed of detail which is both authentic in its own right and quick at every point with the highly individual quality of the author's mind. This is particularly evident in the pace with which details follow one another. They tumble out with unforced vivacity, products of an endless energy. And they exhibit the peculiar violence of White's imagination which is capable of informing the mildest symptom of character or the most delicate indication of place with a strange intensity.

Not all the stories, naturally, are on the same level. The best are 'Down at the Dump', 'The Woman who wasn't Allowed to Keep Cats', 'A Cheery Soul'. 'Willy-Wagtails by Moonlight', designed to exhibit with an almost Somerset Maugham kind of cynicism that people are not always what they appear to be, is altogether too neat and deficient in White's characteristic resonance and seriousness. 'Miss Slattery and her Demon Lover' is a fine, flourishing cartoon of a story with a conventionally eccentric Hungarian, an ordinary loose Australian girl, and a context of a somewhat dandruffed Bohemia. 'Dead Roses' and 'Clay', one about an unawakened and emotionally oppressed girl, the other about what one can only call in an unkind but appropriate way, a compulsive loony, seem designed as comments on D.H. Lawrence's motto in his posthumous essay 'Education of the People',[1] 'down with mothers'. They convey a kind of personal disrelish and they seem to attribute to the mother in each case, a malformation of the subject's nature and brutality in dealing with it on the part of the parent as a kind of effect and cause instead of, perhaps, as cause and effect. Each of these two, the beefy, Betjeman-type Anthea Scudamore and the poor, deluded obsessionist Clay, are altogether too passive and malleable to engage the reader's interest in anything more than a mildly observant way. They are specimens rather than subjects, and while the two worlds in which they live are depicted with characteristic energy and significance, the one distinctly upper, the other lower class, the central figures are altogether too weak and limp. Each story appears to have a vacancy at a point where it should pulse with life.

Perhaps I could illustrate from these stories two unattractive defects which are more obtrusive in the short stories, where they cannot be lost in a longer, more complex movement. Here, for example, from 'Dead Roses', are a few lines which illustrate White rubbing gratingly on the reader's sensibility and calling his attention to the effect in an altogether too ostentatious way:

> It was only the receptacle of which she was in desperate need, in which her uncommunicative nature might spill itself, if silently. So she was hungrily grateful for this stone cell, for the sound of the bent tea-tree as it sawed at iron and silence. And sawed. (p. 19)

That 'And sawed' is a calamitous application of a device White sometimes uses with success in the novels; and so is the apparent precision of the concluding phrase in the following lines, which are clearly intended to pin down and refine the meandering course of Clay's illusion:

Then she came towards him, and he saw that she herself might sink in the waters of time she spread before him cunningly the nets of water smelling of nutmeg over junket the steamy mornings and the rather shivery afternoons. (p. 132)

'And sawed' and 'the rather shivery afternoons' are White at his more relaxed and careless.

A more impressive Australian story, 'The Letters', is the tale of a dim, dry creature, Charles Polkinghorn, who slips more and more away from the roughness of life into some terrifying remoteness. Charles's life, and the influence on it of his self-entranced mother, both indicated with tactful economy, are most intimately and subtly displayed. Her grandeur is that of the self-deifying; her possessions, including her son, are exquisite and cared for because they are hers, perhaps because they are her. The withdrawal of Charles from family, work and life is most convincingly insinuated in the quietest, mildest manner, which makes the horrifying conclusion when the fifty-year-old man is reduced to nuzzling his horrified mother's breasts, more acceptable and inevitable than the equally horrifying conclusion of 'Clay', which has about it something gratuitous and ostentatious.

Most of these stories deal, as do some of the major novels, with afflicted human nature, with the wound in the mind or the burn in the soul. But whereas in the novels the deprivation, or wretchedness, or imperfection becomes a means towards another and deeper reality, in most of the short stories the malady or calamity is part of a self-enclosed system. Neither in 'Clay' nor 'Dead Roses', nor 'The Letters', nor 'A Cheery Soul' do we have that drama of dialectic we find in the novels. The effect in most of these is, however complex, essentially single in its impact, and the only value released appears to be a quality of intensity for its own sake. This is true even of so fine a story as 'A Cheery Soul'. Miss Docker is one whose goodness is a disease. Her sickness is doing good to others. She is indeed a monster, and her monstrosity is made all the more appalling by the accuracy, sometimes the savage accuracy, with which her surroundings are conveyed: the little suburban house where she goes to live with the taciturn Ted Custance and his generous wife, the old people's home where she goes to continue her devastation after being turned out finally by the worn-out Custances, and the church where she succeeds in destroying a clergyman. Here, for example, are some lines which combine clinical accuracy and disgust:

> The whole of Sarsaparilla knew something of Miss Docker's present circumstances: how, since old Miss Baskerville died, and the niece had decided *Lyme Regis* must be sold, there was Miss Docker, soon to find herself without a roof. Almost everyone had been the object of the poor woman's thoughtfulness. One need only mention the Christmas presents she could not afford. Miss Docker was a gift to the gift-shops: all those little ash-trays with gum-nuts in relief, the shepherdesses of dusty lace, the miniature boomerangs, with the holes to hold the toothpicks, to spear the chipolatas with. Everybody knew, but almost everybody forgot. It was more convenient to remember she had her pension and her health. (p. 151)

Miss Docker in her relations with the Custances provides a comedy of desperation:

> 'For some time,' Miss Docker said, 'I have wondered why, amongst good friends, there seems to be a ban on Christian names.'
> Ted Custance could have been warding it off.
> 'I was christened Gertrude,' Miss Docker told. 'But everybody calls me Gee. Gee would feel she really was your friend to hear her name occasionally.'
> Mrs Custance hung her head.
> 'I expect we are not that kind,' she confessed. 'We are not exactly cold people, not formal in any way, but stiff' – here she made the greatest effort – 'yes, I suppose, too, we are shy.'
> 'A name is friendship's sweetener,' Miss Docker coaxed.
> Mr Custance was sweating.
> 'I'm buggered if I will!' he said, very quiet, and quickly went outside. (pp. 160–1)

In the old people's home the play of desperation becomes a farce of destructive cruelty. In the church the comedy becomes one of discrepancy carried to a violent extreme, and in fact the comic is quite absorbed in the horror of destruction. But Miss Docker remains at the end what she began as, a monster without insight, a hero of destruction and a kind of martyr to negation.

Good as 'A Cheery Soul' is, an even better achievement is the group of Greek stories, 'A Glass of Tea', 'The Evening at Sissy Kamara's', 'Being Kind to Titina' and 'The Woman who wasn't Allowed to Keep Cats'. I do not know any modern writer who has been more successful in illuminating the opacity of the Mediterranean world, at least in its Greek aspects. It is a world scored by lines of discrepancy and incomprehension; the men divided from the women, the children from the parents, the visitor from the inhabitant. Never were Greeks so unclassical as these, altogether lacking, as they are, in coolness, coherence and austerity. They are either fractious and nervy, or indolent and abstracted, or blithely, self-centredly crazy. Europe in them seems to be shading into some remoter terrain. Malliakas in 'A Glass of Tea' finds, for example, 'that every Swiss seemed to have achieved a balance, while he, the Greek, could only oppose his undemonstrable inner life and a certain soft elegance' (p. 89). The comparatively calm, commonsensical young man who tells the story in the beautifully organised tale 'Being Kind to Titina' is transformed into 'the awkward thing of flesh' (p. 199) which his childhood acquaintance Titina Stavridi, now an accomplished *putain*, had once been, changing, among shouting uncles and neurotic aunts, into something as tense and feverish as they.

> Outside, the lilac-bushes were turned solid in the moonlight. The white music of that dusty night was frozen in the parks and gardens. As I leaned out of the window, and held up my throat to receive the knife, nothing happened. Only my Aunt Thalia continued playing Schumann, and I realized that my extended throat was itself a stiff sword. (p. 205)

These characters show a glittering surface and a tremblingly vulnerable centre. They cannot bear to be ordinary. ' "Average!" screeched Sissy Kamara, with an expression of triumph and a gold bridge. "Who is average?" ' (p. 143). The women have a hectic, feverish air; the men are remote or passive; each kind is a stranger to the other except for love: 'Often Poppy Pantzopoulos refused to forgive her husband's still perfect profile until she found it on her pillow' (p. 135). The air is melancholy, reminiscent, the memories dominated by Smyrna and the Catastrophe, things dusted with nostalgia assume a vaguely religious aspect: 'Poppy Pantzopoulos had remembered the drawing-room on Frankish Street, the summer stealing through iron shutters, by stealth of light and grace of jasmine, to flirt with the neo-Byzantine plate' (p. 140).

Perhaps the finest of these Greek stories is 'The Woman who wasn't Allowed to Keep Cats', in which Mr and Mrs Spiro Hajistavros, the owners of restaurants and cadillacs in the United States, are reduced on their return to Greece to being simply 'Maro and Spiro, a couple of Greeks' come to visit Mrs Hajistavros's childhood friend, now Mrs Alexiou. This story brilliantly evokes the intense and disappointed memories of the two women, Mrs Alexiou's roof flat with its permanent smell of cat, her ludicrously intellectual husband, and the poor, rich Greek-American husband who 'would have liked to live at peace with all men, but was continually brought to a halt on the edge of a hostile country, partly obscure, partly lambent, which he would end by recognising as the human mind' (p. 248). With what clinical nicety the indolent intellectual is evoked:

> Aleko Alexiou was staring out to sea. He had allowed wind and sunlight to prepare his head for sacrifice.
> 'Take nature,' Alexiou said.
> His hand was helping him extract, or mould, a painfully refractory object.
> 'Nature is so – so – *un*-coo*p*erative, ultimately so *unreal!*'
> Then his hand fell, and with it his failure, while the illusory light continued to cascade into a spurious sea. (pp. 263–4)

This middle-class Mediterranean world of poverty and pretension, of natures both exquisite and brutal, of aspiration which wholly ignores reality, is conveyed with an extraordinary inwardness and conviction. Its melancholy, its bared human nerves, its direct and powerful tradition, its truth of resistance to the modern world: all these are conveyed with an amazing and creative accuracy.

The finest story in *The Burnt Ones* is 'Down at the Dump', a complex lyrical piece, engaging much that is best and most authentic in White's talent, and a triumph of sensibility which, as Henry James says, 'Takes to itself the faintest hints of life [and] converts the very pulses of the air into revelation'. The story is set in Sarsaparilla between a 'red brick propriety' on the one side, occupied by Councillor and Mrs Hogben and their daughter Meg who had 'the eyes of a mopey cat', and the gray, unpainted weatherboard of the Whalleys who were in the bits-and-pieces trade. Everything associated with these people is astonishingly eloquent of character and ethos. The Hogbens' liver-coloured brick house had not a single damp mark on the ceiling, nor, one is sure, is there a mark of any kind on the washing machine, the septic, the TV, the cream Holden Special, or the telephone, kept swabbed with Breath-o'-Pine. And Wal Whalley had a better eye than anyone for the things a person really needs: '. . .dead batteries and musical bedsteads, a carpet you wouldn't notice was stained, wire, and again wire, clocks only waiting to jump back into the race of time' (p. 284). If the Whalleys (Wal is still a fairly appetising male, the children had inherited their mother's colour, 'and when they stood together, golden-skinned, tossing back their unmanageable hair, you would have said a mob of taffy brumbies') stand for the richness, health and grossness of life and the Hogbens for meanness and deprivation, skinny young Meg in her cramped school uniform and surly Lum Whalley with his dreams of driving through the night in his own truck, or at least a semi-trailer, represent possibilities of renewal. Lum and Meg's first awkward interrogation of each other takes place at the Sarsaparilla dump, separated from Sarsaparilla cemetery only by a few strands of barbed wire, while the interment of Mrs Whalley's sister Daise is proceeding. The dump itself heaves with a strange, sprawling life:

> Here and there it appeared as though trash might win. The onslaught of metal was pushing the scrub into the gully. But in many secret, steamy pockets, a rout was in progress: seeds had been sown in the lumps of grey, disintegrating kapok and the laps of burst chairs, the coils of springs, locked in the spirals of wirier vines, had surrendered to superior resilience. (p. 295)

Another and purer stage of existence is implied in the vividly summoned life of Daise, the dead woman whose morals may have been loose but whose feelings were generous and tender, whether for the man who kept her or for the repulsive, deadbeat Ossie whom she wheeled home from the dump in a wheel barrow one night and nourished with food, sex and Franciscan compassion.

Not, I hasten to add, that 'Down at the Dump' is in any way marked by a banal and static symbolism. Wal is really a dustman, Councillor Hogben a creepy politician, Meg a genuine schoolgirl. It is just that the things, the people, the location, all the items and gear of the fiction, carry a spontaneous, flowing significance. Moreover, the radically disjunctive consciousness, the intuition of grace and life, frequently succumbing to or only occasionally resisting the calculated, discursive and Benthamite mentality, which makes for an absolute division in some of the work, operates here in a subtler, altogether more poetically concrete way.

This story, like the best of White's achievement, springs from a pure sense of existence, which stretches in its sympathy from the dense and dirty embodiments of existence in the haphazard gear of the rubbish dump, through every kind of modulation of life up to a level of experience which is spiritual in its candour and fineness. I have called Patrick White a traditional artist. But this is not to declare that in discriminating grades of existence he freezes them into any falsely static posture. He is not in that sense a hierarchical writer. On the contrary, there is a constant touching of different worlds, a Lawrentian sort of mobility and flow. A point of contrast becomes a point of connection. The rubbish dump in 'Down at the Dump' runs into the cemetery. The voice of goodness from the grave calls out to the devious town councillor. It is among the heaving rubbish of the dump that the young lovers make their first tender inquiries of one another. The mystery of existence, the mystery of self, the mutuality of experience and self – this 'metaphysical' theme, no more than hinted at here – rolls like a profound current all through Patrick White's work. This depth of preoccupation is the animating presence which quickens the multiplying details and orders the vast range of material in the fiction (but also, and not infrequently, which clouds the clues the artist offers to what he is about with too large and unmanageable a significance).

Just as 'Down at the Dump', simple and brief as it is, involves in undertone and suggestion Patrick White's preoccupation with being, so too it is constantly in touch, at least in hint and intimation, with the other sustaining theme of his fiction – the exploration of self. His precise interest in this short story is one that a distinction of Coleridge lights up: '. . .self – i.e. the image or complex cycle of imagination. . .which is the perpetual representative of our Individuum. . .'². Patrick White is concerned in miniature in 'Down at the Dump', *in extenso* in the novels, with all the subtleties of relationship between individuality and the self.

The six *novellas* and short stories in *The Cockatoos* (1975), varying in location from Sicily to Sydney, show Patrick White, if not absolutely at the pitch of his powers – since this would require a richer orchestration of theme and a larger area to manoeuvre in – certainly as possessed as ever of a ferocity of communicating skill, and as capable of constructing from common and dandruffed material a world which is rhapsodic and realistic. There is the same flow of creative capacity that one sees in the major novels, which can find, in situations of a seedy simplicity and characters of conventional mediocrity, subjects and themes of depth and urgency. The manner combines the more nearly abstinent idiom developed about the period of *The Solid Mandala* with the endless, burrowing, spiritual inquisitiveness so characteristic of the mature work. The stories are told with a straighter narrative, a more regular syntax, and a much less drowning torrent of metaphor. But there is still the accustomed ease and flow of imaginative energy.

There is, indeed, one positive advantage in these stories in that they head off White's occasional inability to resist gratuitous and unnecessary symbolism, of the kind, for example, which marred significant junctures in *Voss* and *Riders in the Chariot*. In the short stories, or in most of them, the movement between idea and material is vital and unbroken, the theme as intimate with the material as soul with body.

When I spoke of a celebration both lyrical and terrifying, I had in mind once again the binomial or rather, since one feels something tearing and intense in the artist's reaction, the Manichaean nature of Patrick White's sensibility. On one side is the flow of love and grace brilliantly exemplified in the clouds of birds glittering in the neglected suburban gardens in 'The Cockatoos', or the sudden, Franciscan flood of pity and love felt by the brutally delinquent Felicity for the dying derelict in 'The Night the Prowler', or the similar surge of devotion which the elderly, widowed Mrs Natwick feels for her cocky little friend in 'Five-Twenty', or the subdued saintliness of Dowson in 'A Woman's Hand'. On the other, there is the dialectic of loathing expressed in the appalling horrors of the flesh, like the loathsome sex in 'Sicilian Vespers': 'Like two landed fish, they were lunging together, snout bruising snout, on the rucked-up Cosmati paving' (p. 243).

Part of the same idiom is the constant reference, both expressed and metaphorical, to what is raw, ugly, or offensive. Patrick White has always made great play in his work with such elements in Australian provincial life, which often serves as a baseline against which the reader is to measure simplicity and goodness. But where these things once filled him with mockery or bitterness, they now suffuse him wth disgust and despair. Stench, slime, mucus, excrement, decay, the ruined body – these are notes very often touched on in these stories. Even a meal in a restaurant assumes an appearance of horrors: 'There were some splinters of fish done in sawdust. She refused to wrestle with her cartilage of mutton. Over their helpings of marshmallow and tinned pineapple-ring the honeymoon couples were beginning to uncoil' (p. 83); and when a candle burns in church in the Greek war story 'The Full Belly', it is anaemic 'amongst the grubby pellets, the sickly stalactites, of last year's wax' (p. 115).

White in these shorter works, as in the major novels, shows himself not greatly concerned with originality in situation or character. The situation in most of these stories is orthodox, even traditional. An officious wife tries to arrange a marriage for her husband's friend, a Greek family looks for food under the German occupation, a young woman experiences an unsuccessful rape, birds visit and then invade a neighbourhood and the lives of the neighbours, a widow's new friend is killed by a car, two married couples meet as tourists in Sicily, a teenage girl turns to violence.

For most novelists these are circumstances and people which would pretty firmly limit treatment and development, but Patrick White's extraordinary skill allows them to become – I put it like this because his treatment, once seen, seems inevitable –

monstrous and illuminating. Like the pianist with his piano in 'The Full Belly' he turns this 'furniture into instrument'. One cannot too highly praise, for example, his power of representation, the conviction of his surfaces, textures, implied depths. At the same time, his incessant interrogation of every form of existence gives to the dense reality of things and persons an intellectual and imaginative buoyancy. Everything moves, there is no arrest in personality, existence glides and turns and flows. What we see in these stories is the process of *becoming*. White's art is at the other extreme from the static, his universe – like the relations of his characters – melting and modulating at every point.

The stories in *The Cockatoos* are the product of a powerful and singular literary personality. At its centre is a vision of the violence of existence, of the intensity of being itself; and it is rendered with an astonishing energy of realisation. I have perhaps stressed unduly the separation in his vision, the divorce of grace and horror. It might be added that it shows itself in a more than usual share of the current awareness of the nastiness of certain spheres of experience, particularly in matters of sex, and a fierce disdain of the middling and the commonplace – aristocratic characteristics that White shares with Eliot. This argues, I think, a certain failure or distortion in the range of his sympathy for human nature and experience. Perhaps it is a deficiency in our civilisation forcing itself into the artist's work and revealing itself in deficiencies of tact and grasp, as well as in a certain lack of tenderness toward the language.

But at its most mature (as in *Voss* some of these stories come close to belonging to that category, particularly 'Sicilian Vespers', 'The Cockatoos', 'The Full Belly', and 'Five-Twenty'), White's art is quickened and unified by the most powerful and creative quarter of his sensibility, namely a concept of goodness which depends upon an unspoiled wholeness of the person. Such goodness, although it may be striven for, cannot be deserved. It is a stroke of providence or a form of genius, but in any case a gift, a grace, and one most likely to be found in the possession of those commonly regarded as blemished or eccentric or hateful, like Voss, or Theodora Goodman, or Arthur Brown in *The Solid Mandala*. In Patrick White's eyes the supreme gift of man, existing in a context of surliness, ugliness and cruelty, is precisely this clarified consciousness. It is something which belongs above all to those he called 'the poor unfortunates' in the epigraph of his other book of short stories, *The Burnt Ones*. There is a sufficient presence of the burnt ones, the poor unfortunate ones, in *The Cockatoos* to justify, to put into place, the monstrous horrors of human living, of which this sumptuous and tortured talent is harshly conscious.

So much of the action in Patrick White's novels is internally generated, so many distinctive idioms are managed so successfully, so often the vivid surface detail connects naturally with serious and even profound themes, that one might well have expected – apart from his known personal predilection for the theatre, as I pointed out before – had he lived in a country and at a time when the institution of drama thrived, that he would have devoted considerably more of his mind and art to the drama. In fact, four of his plays have been produced in Australia and appeared in print in 1965 (a very early one, *Return to Abyssinia*, of which no copy survives, was put on in London in 1947 and called by *The Times* 'a disarmingly ingenuous little play'). The most dramatically effective of them, at least so far as one can tell from the printed page, is *The Ham Funeral* which was written in 1947 before his novelist's gift had fully formed, and produced in Australia in 1961. In this play White has been more successful than in the others in subordinating the natural intrusiveness of the novelist, particularly one with so peremptory and overwhelming a talent as his own. Nevertheless, one can see from the stage directions the bias of the novelist, which is to make himself more actively present than as a dramatist he should. Here are two short excerpts from the stage directions in *The Ham Funeral*:

> Before the CURTAIN rises, the YOUNG MAN appears, and speaks the following prologue. He is dressed informally, in a fashion which could be about 1919. He is rather pale. His attitude throughout the play is a mixture of the intent and the absent, aggressiveness and diffidence.

> The LANDLORD is seated on one of the deal chairs beside the kitchen table. He sits with his legs apart, facing the

audience. He is a vast man, swollen, dressed from neck to ankle in woollen underclothes, of a greyish colour, and in carpet slippers. His face is pallid, flushing to strawberry in the nose, and in a wen on one cheek. He wears a thick, drooping moustache, and is smoking a short, black pipe. The LANDLADY is also seated at the kitchen table, with a saucepan, peeling potatoes. She is a large woman in the dangerous forties, ripe and bursting. Her hair, still black, is swept up untidily in a vaguely Edwardian coiffure. She is wearing a shabby white satin blouse, dark skirt, and an old pair of pink mules. LANDLADY continues to peel potatoes, but with mounting boredom and distaste.

These passages themselves seem to me to demonstrate the novelist's passion to be seen mastering the material and ordering each step and shade in the action. And, indeed, all the plays suggest a certain lack of confidence on the part of the dramatist in his actors and partners. Drama as a collaboration is something very hard for the novelist to accept.

White as dramatist, then, asks for a very exact and even finicky correspondence with his intentions. He also avails himself of the poetic and technical devices reintroduced into the theatrical repertoire by the German Expressionists. Now, of course, one finds them perfectly acceptable and even conventional, although one feels, particularly in *A Cheery Soul* and *The Season at Sarsaparilla*, a degree of discomfort in the passage from the allegorical to the representational manner. In *The Ham Funeral*, however, there is a much more natural flow between the two sides. The play is set in some vaguely London scene – really, simply in a place – in a crummy boarding house kept by Alma Lusty (even the names are somewhat obviously made to work for the theme), who is driven by an uncomprehended rage for life, and her reticent husband, Will, whose death is the main event in the play.

One of the lodgers is the young man, whose progress from fastidious, willed detachment to a more naturally and exclusive implication provides the dramatic mobility of the piece. The other side of the young man's self, his anima, or image as Coleridge puts it, is projected on to a dreary fellow lodger, Phyllis Pither. As the anima, the girl is romantic and reminiscent of the figure

in Eliot's 'Marina' (indeed, there are several hints of Eliot in
the play as one would expect from the period); as Phyllis she
is a limp creature with a cold. Will, an ex-wrestler, philosopher,
and finally silent contemplator of reality, dies – we do not know
why, although explanations are offered during the ham tea, one
even being that Mrs Lusty is responsible. The young man rejects
the advances of the writhing Alma, although this is not proposed
as any final rejection of life but rather as a stage of his journey
towards maturity and completeness. The romantic ideal represented by the young woman, who leaves a sprig of lilac as an
earnest of her reality, is a trifle thin and Rossetti-like. But there
is also some superb comedy in the play, particularly a splendid
scene in which the young man on his way to inform Will's
relatives of his death, discovers two old ladies rummaging in the
dust bins in search of bits and pieces which we realise are very
much more than what they seem. And the ham tea itself after
the funeral has a positively Chaucerian vitality and thrust.

   The Ham Funeral seems to me an economically organised
and highly actable play, both theatrically and dramatically
effective, and managed both with instinct and skill. Its deficiency,
which is one rarely associated with White's major work, is a
certain attenuated and misty quality in the central experience,
reminiscent of *The Living and the Dead*. That is certainly not
a charge that could be levelled at *The Season at Sarsaparilla*,
which is described as 'A Charade of Suburbia in Two Acts'. This
is a robust and energetic play, but to me it is strangely lacking
in those skills of dramatic management evident in *The Ham
Funeral*. The half dozen principal characters are, in this context,
not only orthodox but conventional. Even the little girl, Pippy
Pogson, whom White describes in his novelist's way in the stage
directions as 'a forthright and astute small girl', is more of a
camera eye than a living person. (Compare her, for example,
in respect of complexity and conviction with Maisie in Henry
James's *What Maisie Knew*. How thin, and merely perky she
is!) The males, whether of the office or the manual kind, and
the women, whether refined or earthy, are generalised in their
ordinariness. The two dim young men, one decent and one
romantic, again are gestures towards personalities. The point of
the contrast between a natural, breathing vitality and the clich
és of suburbia are hammered home with a repetitive and unsubtle

emphasis. The pack of dogs in pursuit of a bitch in heat, howling intermittently through the play, which so much engages Pippy Pogson, who was beginning to sniff at the facts of life, are a raucous and somewhat too obvious device.

The set of contrasts which constitute the substance of the play, between suburbia and life, between the artistic and the commonplace, between man and his man-made wilderness, between the Australian pastoral myth and its huddled actuality, between mateship and lust, are not articulated with White's customary mastery but lie lumpily side by side. Nor has the language that resonance and evocative power which it so often has in the novels. Here is a characteristic passage in which Nola Boyle, the unfaithful wife of Ernie the sanitary man, expresses her kind of self-indulgent and slouching sensuality:

> Nola (*strolling, picking at this and that in the garden, smelling here and there at a flower, soliloquising*) This is the best time of all. Before the men come. (*However, she looks at her watch*) Even in summer, at the end of the day, when you feel you could have been spat out, when the hair is stuck to your forehead, it is best, best. A time to loiter. The flowers are lolling. The roses are biggest. (*Stoops to smell*) The big, lovely roses, falling with one touch. . . (*Laughs*) I could eat the roses! Dawdling in the back yard. If there was none of these busybodies around (*glancing at the Pogson home*) – thin, prissy, operated women – I'd take off me clothes, and sit amongst the falling roses. I've never felt the touch of roses on my body. (*Examining her bare arm*) Green in the shade. Green for shade. Splotchy. You can imagine the petals, trickling, trickling, better than water, because solid. . . (*She looks again at her watch, irritation rising*) But the men don't come! They gotta come! When you expect them. Now, or then, it's the same. They gotta come. The men. Standing in bars, with arms round one another's shoulders, faces running together, to tell a bluer story. . . Men are dirty buggers! But they oughta come. They're expected. (pp. 125–6)

The combination of realistic and non-realistic techniques works uncomfortably in the suburban scene, which seems much more naturally made for a more caustic kind of realism. The play is episodic rather than organic in its development, and the themes a set of abstract convictions applied to rather than drawn out of the situation.

In two of the most intelligent treatments of White's plays, that by Barry Argyle[3] and that by R. F. Brissenden,[4] a similar point is made. Here is the shorter and clearer version of it given by Brissenden:

> At the risk of gross oversimplification one can, I think, isolate these two centres of interest in White's plays: on the one hand the individual, struggling to come to terms with himself and with the universe in which he lives – a universe in which inanimate objects and the world of nature can be as important as other human beings; and on the other the cyclic processes of living, impersonal, inscrutable, and inescapable. Dramatic tensions and interests are generated in his work not only out of the relationship of the characters with each other (as in the case of most plays) but also out of their involvement with these larger biological and physical forces.

This seems to me an admirable expression of White's dramatic intentions, more fully realised in *The Ham Funeral*, less adequately substantiated in the other three plays. In the drama more than any other literary form, ideas and themes must be, in Coleridge's word, 'impersonated'. The season in the title and the howling pack of dogs after the bitch in heat in the play *The Season at Sarsaparilla*, not to speak of other theatrical devices like the gauzily, filmy back-presence of Mrs Lillie's youth in *A Cheery Soul*, are wholly insufficient substitutes for actual, dramatic embodiment. They tend, rather, to give the impression of a novelist desperately seeking to reproduce on the stage the wider and subtler effects that his words are capable of suggesting in the novel.

The dramatised version of *A Cheery Soul* illustrates this employment of inappropriate techniques and irrelevant kinds of subtlety. In *A Cheery Soul* the necessary element of conflict exists theoretically between Miss Docker's insensitive passion to help her neighbours and some more balanced concept of neighbourliness. She illustrates one side of the opposition, but nothing 'impersonates' the other. Moreover, Miss Docker is a cartoon rather than a character, limited and one-dimensional. *A Cheery Soul* certainly contains some vigorous and pointed scenes but they are in a strict sense farcical rather than comic or tragic. As this play illustrates, White has a brilliant sense for the dramatic situation or moment. The scene in the church between the inarticulate and virtuous clergyman and the bullying goodwill of Miss Docker combines ridicule and pathos in an original and telling way. But such things are momentary and the rest of the play appears simply as an arrangement or context in which dramatic functions may appear, not the irresistible ground for them. The last scene in the play in which a dog urinates on the frustrated Miss Docker's leg, is, like the chorus of howling dogs in *The Season at Sarsaparilla*, another example of willed imagery which cannot support the weight put on it.

The burden of critical opinion on *Night on Bald Mountain* seems to be that it is an impressive but failed tragedy. By tragedy people usually have in mind here the Greek form, a disposition enforced by the pretty exact observance of the unities, the choric function performed by the splendid Miss Quodling, the hints of incest or its surrogate psychological form, the intensity of guilt and the sacrifice of the victim. I find this account of it not so much inadequate as irrelevant. No amount of the application of Greek modes can transform the material of what is essentially a melodrama. Indeed, it seems to me a spirited and fascinating one. The characters are not particularly original but they are individually seized and displayed, the varieties of their suffering are conventionally demonstrated, and above all the language of the play and the idiom of each character are both lively and well fitted. Several critics have noticed how passive the central experience is. Hugo Sword, the Professor of English, is tortured by his own frustrations both scholarly and personal; his wife, the alcoholic Miriam, is tortured by him, and by herself, and by her addiction; Stella Summerhayes, the pretty virgin nurse, is tortured by both. The minor characters, Cantwell a grocer, and the rather dim lecturer Denis Craig, add a touch of realism and imply the existence of another world and other values, but not with sufficient force to make the experience embodied in the Swords's house and family more than an obsessively negative and solipsistic one.

The one vital thing in the play seems to me to be the

language, and the most moving and potent form of it is that of Miss Quodling, whose crackling, racily active speech generates whatever is positive in the play. Too much attention has been paid to its symbolic content and shading. What is splendid about it is its force, raciness and sharpness. Here is her hymn of praise to the morning, with which the play begins:

> Mornun. . .I love it even when it skins yer! Oh, yes, it can hurt!. . .When the ice crackles underfoot. . .and the scrub tears the scabs off yer knuckles. . .and the spiders' webs are spun again. . .first of all. . .out of dew. . .it's to remind that life begins at dawn. Bald Mountain! I wasn't born here. Oh, no! But know it, how I know it! I've learnt to understand the silences of rocks. Only the barren can understand the barren. I came, because I couldn't help it. I tasted the little, runty apples. . .and sour apricots. . .that somebody planted before they died. On Bald Mountain, nobody else has survived. Nobody else. I've lived here so long, I've forgotten now. (*Pause*) I don't go down. . . (*pointing behind her*). . .not down there. . .though I watch the lights. . .at night. . .that glitter too much to be trusted. In the end, you can't trust anythun but goats and silence. Oh, yes, I know now! I've seen the mountain from a distance, too. . .moisture glist'nun on its bald patch. . .on bare rock. Sun on rock. . .that's the kiss that never betrays. . .because it doesn't promise nothun. . .(p. 272)

The truth is that as a dramatist Patrick White is a casualty of the times and of the theatrical tradition in his own country. The living drama of his work is to be found in the novels.

5 *Major Phase II*

To go from *Riders in the Chariot* to *The Solid Mandala* (1966), is to move from a novel which is spacious and inclusive to one in which the field of action is confined, in which the language is more abstinent, the metaphorical habit less florid, the manner altogether trimmer and sharper, and the elements of the 'arrangement, distribution and composition' – as Henry James puts it – are more finely balanced. Moreover, the structure of this novel is more intimately related to its animating idea. The movement between idea and material is vital and unbroken, and there is no sense of supporting scaffolding as there is, one finally feels, in *Riders in the Chariot*. This spare novel – spare by Patrick White's standards, that is – is one of the most beautifully organised of White's works and one marked by an unusual blend of inwardness and control, life and impersonality.

The story begins with a bus journey in which the decent Mrs Poulter and her dim crony, Mrs Dun, circle a place once a village now a suburb, in which the remnants of the country die in the suburban landscape. Bits of ragged greenery and the stench of crushed weeds compete with bush shelters, concrete paving, and council-approved parapets. The Service Station had risen on what had been Allwright's General Store:

> Exhaust fumes and the metallic idiom of mechanics had routed the indolent mornings which used to weigh so heavy on Allwright's buckled veranda, bulging with bags of potatoes and mash, stacked with the boxes of runty tomatoes the growers brought out from under the seats of their sulkies. (p. 60)

The bus journey has in it a certain ritual quality, as though the two ladies are not only beating the bounds of the terrain of the

85

novel but defining its sensibility. What was once the place where a Chinese woman grew vegetables and planted wheel-trees is achieving a glossier life, of picture windows and texture brick. Mrs Poulter and Mrs Dun, in 'the flannelly atmosphere of the bus' (p. 14), finding that 'the private lives of other parties act as the cement of friendship' – a nice touch of White's wit – introduce us to the Brown brothers, 'a couple of no-hopers with ideas about 'emselves, the Brothers Bloody Brown' (p. 18) as Mrs Poulter's husband, the roadsweeper, calls them.

We first see the two old men stumbling along the road between Barranugli and Sarsaparilla, one in a stiff oilskin, the other in a yellowed herringbone tweed. They are hand in hand and accompanied by their blue terriers, Runt and Scruffy. The mere minimum of context is sufficient for White to bring on his main figures, the shambling, simple-minded Arthur Brown, and the brittle, 'gifted' Waldo. The two old men, at once repulsive and appealing, are made unbearably present in their hideous, pitiable humanity, habit lending them substance, and more than habit making them one. The novel swoops backwards and forwards in time from this moment with the fleeting but severe logic of poetry or life. They are handcuffed, as they grope down the path negotiating the irregular bricks, by love and hate, memory and genes, horror and misery. A whole universe is summoned up in the novel's slim beginning, a world which includes the clotted paddocks of Terminus Row, and the world in which people lived, belonged to Fellowships and Lodges, and are not afraid of electric gadgets. That world is the context for the tragedy of the Browns, parents and children, which is itself a comment on the words of Meister Eckhart quoted as an epigraph, 'It is not outside, it is inside: wholly within'. The twins are themselves divided parts of one person, and the tension which divides and unites them dramatises the disturbance within man and within the single person. They act out that impure mixture of love and hate which is both a condition of the relationship of every human being to another and the condition of the attitude of the individual within himself to himself.

The narrative manner of this novel is, as in all White's major work, thick with explicit particulars. Everything is embodied and illustrated. Each shade of feeling or quirk of action is solidly realised. But the narrative technique is more mobile than, although just as coherent as, the usual biographical line favoured by White. The narrative technique – that is the way the novel thinks, the way the work is conscious – swoops and turns and flicks from point to point, with a logic different from that of simple sequence. There is a splendid passage in Lawrence's introduction to his translation of *Cavalleria Rusticana* which relates White's technique here to the movement of the emotional mind:

> Now the emotional mind, if we may be allowed to say so, is not logical. It is a psychological fact, that when we are thinking emotionally or passionately, thinking and feeling at the same time, we do not think rationally: and therefore, and therefore, and therefore. Instead, the mind makes curious swoops and circles. It touches the point of pain or interest, then swoops and circles, coils round and approaches again the point of pain or interest. . .[1]

In *The Solid Mandala* the procedure is one of shading and emphasis, of varying the point of entrance and sweeping backwards and forwards in a way which impresses the reader as a composition rather than a linear progress. The actual structure of the novel is composed of a series of similar movements or concentric circles. The outermost one is made up of ordinary people like Mrs Poulter and Mrs Dun and the whole community of Sarsaparilla. Inside that there is the tighter circle of the Brown family, and within that again the more intense circle of the brothers, and within that again the light-imprisoning, solid mandala itself. This was Arthur's favourite among the four permanencies he had as a boy, one gold, one cloudy blue, one whorled with green, and one, the mandala, a taw with a knot at the centre. When he grew up he stutteringly read in an encyclopaedia belonging to the husband of the rich Mrs Musto:

> '*The Mandala is a symbol of totality. It is believed to be the "dwelling of the god". Its protective circle is a pattern of order super – imposed on – psychic – chaos. Sometimes its geometric form is seen as a vision (either waking or in a dream) or –*'
> His voice had fallen to the most elaborate hush.
> (*Or danced*), Arthur read. (p. 238)

Perhaps I can comment on each of these in turn. The narrative mode of this novel, having benefited, surely, from the discipline of the plays and short stores, is altogether quieter, more collected, and the clarity of the medium allows affective scope to Patrick White's gift for producing a richly orchestrated actuality, an actuality which includes both an accurate surface and the whole net of the implicit and significant trailing beneath it. In this part of the novel we have not only the exact registration of the physical appearance of the place, but also a sense of the community's reaction, its ethos and feeling. There is considerable stress on the rougher and more abrasive elements of Australian common life. The names of the people and places, for example, are redolent of a kind of truculent glumness: Wally Pugh, Mrs Purves, Mrs Musto, Mr Mutton, Norm Croucher, the dogs Scruffy and Runt, O'Halloran Road, Ada Avenue, Sarsaparilla, Barranugli, Shadbolt Lane, Gippa Gunyan, Mungindribble. The ugliness these names stand for is confirmed by the half-aggressive idiom which is the common idiom of communication and the two together convey, negatively and positively, the feeling of a society which is both traditionally and visually uneducated, and possessed of an openness and freedom untrammelled by the weight of any oppressive inheritance. As Mr Brown said once to Waldo and Arthur, 'There's too much you boys, reared in the light in an empty country, will never understand. There aren't any shadows in Australia. Or discipline. Every man jack can do what he likes' (p. 161).

The members of the shadowless, unencumbered community are given a solid, compelling existence, whether they are casual figures glimpsed for a moment, like Waldo's colleagues seen in the Municipal Library, or the Allwrights who keep a shop Arthur works in, or the Misses Dallimores, the local snobs, or the rich eccentric Mrs Musto, or whether they are more fully developed like the immediate neighbours of the Brown family, the dull, decent Poulters or the Feinstein family who, with their Jewish cultivation and intelligence, bring to the general British surliness a further note of comparative definition. The community's response to the Browns' tragedy, Arthur's simple-mindedness, varies between the horror of worried parents when Arthur is young – "I warn yer, Mr Brown," Mr Haynes was saying, and his usually jolly chins were compressed, "you'll have to restrain him. Yer don't realise a big lump of a boy like that can turn violent. In his condition. It's hard, I know, for the parents to see." (p. 47) – to the exaggerated bonhommie of the men hiding their embarrassment at the Speedex Service Station when Arthur is old – 'Hi, mate! Hi, Arthur! How's the Brown Bomb?' (p. 59).

Caustic as White's attitude may be towards what one can only call the commonality of Sarsaparilla (though it is frequently a very witty disdain), he manifests towards the Brown parents, living a life of marriage of dumb disappointment as well as one increasingly on the lip of despair, a measured and delicate compassion. To the chronic misery of their life, hopes destroyed, gentility bruised, a remorseless decline in status, polite poverty, the Browns add the painful tragedy of their simpleton son. The well-bred Mrs Brown, born a Quantrell, who had long stopped calling tea 'dinner', had Married Beneath Her, continued to love her husband, and Arthur the afflicted son, and continued to try to love Waldo. 'Her pure, inherited voice erected a barrier not only between herself and Mrs Poulter, but those she had conceived in an adulterated tradition' (p. 73). Her nerves continued to be frayed by the realities of a working-class life. Poor Mr Brown, a man of principle and kindness as his wife explained when he died, club-footed, an unconstructed Pom, had the taste but neither the opportunity nor the intellect for the intellectual life. He insists to the puzzled builder of his house on having a classical pediment stuck illogically on its roof. His working life was spent in conscientious wretchedness as a clerk in the bank, and his increasingly hostile schoolboy son Waldo, a Promising Lad, would accompany him on the train to Sydney each morning. There is sour comedy and savage pathos in George Brown's effort to communicate with Waldo on these occasions, in the intervals, incidentally, of learning Norwegian in order to be able to read Ibsen in the original.

> 'Waldo, I've been meaning to have a talk. For some time. About certain things. About, well, life. And so forth.'
> The spidery train was clutching at the rails. The smuts flew in, to sizzle on Waldo's frozen skin.
> 'Because,' continued George Brown, 'I expect there are things that puzzle you.'

Nhoooh! Waldo might have hooted if the engine hadn't beaten him to it.

It wasn't the prospect of his father's self-exposure which was shaking him. It was the train, shaking out every swollen image he had ever worked on.

'The main thing,' said Dad, sucking his sparrow-coloured moustache, 'is to lead a decent, a life you, well, needn't feel ashamed of.'

O Lord. Waldo had not been taught to pray, because, said Mother, everything depends on your own will, it would be foolishness to expect anything else, we can achieve what we want if we are determined, if we are confident that we are strong.

And here was George Brown knotting together the fingers which had learnt to handle the pound notes so skilfully. Who had nothing to feel ashamed of. Except perhaps his own will.

O Lord. The Barranugli train bellowed like a cow in pastures not her own.

'For instance, all these diseases.' George Brown found himself looking at his own flies. He looked away.

Waldo, though he did not want to, could not help looking at his father, at the sweat shining on the yellow edge of his celluloid collar.

'There's a bit of advice, Waldo,' he was saying, 'I'd like to give any boy. You can't be too careful of those lavatory seats, I mean, the public lavatories. You can develop, well, a technique of balance. And avoid a lot of trouble. That Way.' (pp. 77–8)

More deeply affecting is the sense of the Browns' tragedy communicated in the scene where Waldo remembers as an old man the last visit they paid as children to the bank where their father worked:

. . .Waldo noticed their father looking out from the cage in which he stood: the citron-coloured face, its seams nicked by the cut-throat with flecks of black, morning blood, the moustache, interesting to touch before it had grown raggedy. Their father's eyes were brown, which Arthur had inherited. Their father's stare was at that moment directed outward, and not. He had not yet developed his asthma, though might have that morning in the tearing silence of the brown bank. Suddenly his shoulders hunched, to resist, it seemed, compression by the narrow cage, his eyes were more deeply concentrated on some invisible point. More distinctly even than the morning he found their father dead Waldo would remember the morning of their last visit to the bank. (p. 54)

The father and the mother, both so English in their different ways, the one clogged 'in an impasto of nonconformist guilt', the other, before she takes to the sweet sherry bottle in old age, one of those vaguely upper-class figures that Patrick White does so well, who seem in the modern urban British scene in fact quite as strange as they were in Sarsaparilla. Nourished by the most anaemic abstractions of high-minded rationalism and genteel socialism the Brown parents live a dumbly desperate life, balancing in the air – just – their hopeless aspirations, their painful memories, their present disappointments, their insoluble problems with the twins.

The parents are revealed in their shabby nakedness, and there is no burking or fudging or turning away in White's scrutiny of them, and yet the attitude manifested has in it no touch of that gratuitous cruelty or attraction to the repulsive which sometimes disfigures the clarity of the novelist's feelings. Each in his limited way is a good person, each is a failure, each inadequate for the strains put upon them. But each, also, is an integral whole, completely human creation, and this quality in the two Brown parents receives from the author the respect it deserves.

It is in this context, this nest as Arthur would sense it, this pit as it seems to Waldo, that the boys develop their afflicted natures, and their ambiguous and cloudy relationships. Arthur, a 'dill', a shingle short, with defective intelligence and speech, blundering and blubbering in physical action, is one whose equipment for life is poverty-stricken beyond the average. He has certain practical abilities. He can milk the cow, make bread – his English father was disgusted at these feminine hobbies – enjoy his work as a delivery boy with the local grocers, is good with animals: 'it was perhaps natural for them to accept someone who was only half a human being'. There is one odd, discrepant fact in Arthur's psychology which, strange as it is, is somehow in keeping with another side of nature. The fact is his uncomprehending prodigy's gift for doing sums at school, a skill which has no connection with intelligence in the ordinary sense. The other side of Arthur's nature is some peculiar sweetness or openness which makes him, with all his incapacities, a positive and protective influence. His mother loves him and he returns that love with the most unaffected candour. Women feel a deep affection for him, particularly Mrs Poulter and Dulcie Feinstein. He can break in, in however fuddled a way, into the lives of others, a gift utterly foreign to his brother. Arthur may not have an intelligence, but he certainly has a soul, and as his life develops he gains a deeper insight into what Lawrence calls 'the realities' or 'the other world of pure being'.[2] Insight is perhaps too cerebral a way to describe Arthur's feeling for the nature of reality. It is both more shapeless and more immediate than this term would suggest. The image of it is his solid mandala, the most mysterious of the glass marbles which he fondles in his pocket and peers into entranced. Arthur contemplates his marble almost in the religious sense, seeing in it mysteries, realities, symbols and significances – an endless range of reality enclosed in a miniature universe.

There is a MS. note of Coleridge quoted by Kathleen Coburn in her anthology *Inquiring Spirit* which I find brilliantly illuminating when I think of the relations of Arthur Brown and his brother:

> Two things we may learn from little children from three to six years old: 1. That it is a characteristic, an instinct of our human nature to pass out of self – i.e. the image or complex cycle of images. . .which is the perpetual representative of our Individuum, and by all unreflecting minds confounded and identified with it,. . .2. Not to suffer any one form to pass into me and become a usurping self.[3]

This general characteristic of mankind, on the one hand a restless search for release from the confinement of the single image of oneself, on the other a solicitude to keep inviolable the privacy of another self, is divided between Arthur and Waldo. Arthur passes almost effortlessly into the lives and feelings of others, but he is entranced by the images of these as he is infatuated with the glints and clouds and lights in his glass marbles. But Waldo carries this fierce sense of his own identity and his resistance to the intrusion of others to a point where it is pathological and, since it is invariably connected with self-love, evil. But each of us is born with an incommunicable core of self. But Waldo carries to extremity this natural bias, he is a spiritual and emotional solipsist. Life and experience seem to him a violation of his enclosed perfection, an assault on his privacy.

Waldo, a bright boy, a promising lad, has all the gifts that Arthur lacks. He is sharp, educated, with a taste for the intellectual life and an aspiration to be a writer. He works in a dreamy, intermittent way on the fragment of a novel, *Tiresias a Youngish Man*. When the children were young, Mrs Brown persuaded herself Arthur was some kind of genius waiting to disclose itself. 'But Dad was not deceived, Waldo even less. Waldo didn't believe it possible to have more than one genius around' (p. 35). He makes ineffectual efforts to enter into relationships with others, with friends at the library, with Walter Pugh, and his relations Cis and Ern, and more agonisingly with the Jewish girl Dulcie Feinstein. But Dulcie, who is a sensitive and sympathetic girl, finds something repellantly icy in Waldo. Even his father's goodness is something Waldo cannot touch. He can only be touched by it. Waldo's is a polished, metallic surface, impermeable to others, whether in the community or the family. Mrs Poulter, for example, 'was one of the 57 things and persons Waldo hated' and 'Waldo liked to look into the houses he passed, obliquely though, for on some of those occasions when he had stared full in he had been faced with displays of perversity to damage temporarily his faith in reason' (pp. 58–9).

Only with Arthur could Waldo begin to touch another. It is true that he would, when there were guests, with candid and unostentatious charity 'which moved the observer – as well as the performer' carefully brush the crumbs which had fallen on Arthur's knees. But 'Life, as he began in time to see it, is the twin consciousness, jostling you, hindering you, but with which, at unexpected moments, it is possible to communicate in ways both animal and delicate' (p. 77). If Waldo was 'truly tortured by the innocence in others to which he was periodically subjected' the reason was as much the otherness as the innocence. Whereas

Arthur contemplates his glass taws, Waldo constantly examined himself in the mirror, engaging in the only relationship which increasingly becomes possible to him, an incestuous relationship with himself. Waldo is a *voyeur* and his closest relationship with his mother is his perverse wearing of her dress after she is dead. Waldo's tragedy is that his natural solipsism, an extreme development of a universal bias, is horrifyingly imperfect from the very beginning of his existence. It is invaded by his twin who is appallingly both himself and another. So that Waldo's life is a living contradiction of his nature.

The result is a hardness of the spirit, or better, the petrification of the faculty of relatedness. It is the tragedy of Waldo's life, therefore, that his very passion to protect the self works against the one reality he is capable of accepting, his own. The isolated individual goes numb since individuality does not consist in a set of characteristics contained within a particular skin but in connection, in growth and elaboration of connection.

> The fact remains [says Lawrence] that when you cut off a man and isolate him in his own pure and wonderful individuality, you haven't got the man at all. You've only got the dreary fag-end of him. . .We have our very individuality in relationship. Let us swallow this important and prickly fact. Apart from our connections with other people, we are barely individuals; we amount, all of us, to next to nothing. It is in the living touch between us and other people, other lives, other phenomena that we move and have our being. Strip us of our human contacts and of contact with the living earth, and we are almost bladders of emptiness.[4]

When Waldo, out of that destructive blend of self-hatred and hatred of others which characterises the neurotic mind, moves from his first library post to the big new public library in Sydney, he uses his considerable skill and intelligence to avoid any living contact with his colleagues. He swerves aside from the gestures made to him by Miss Glasson 'so well balanced in her golfing shoes' (p. 183) and from Cornelius, the ascetic Jew, or straightforward Parslow:

> So Waldo, who was in frequent demand, continued to refuse, on principle, by formula.

To submit himself to the ephemeral, the superficial relationships might damage the crystal core holding itself in reserve for some imminent moment of higher idealism. Just as he had avoided fleshly love – while understanding its algebra, of course – the better to convey eventually its essence. (p. 183)

Even when he decides to be kind, in a period of idealism, and buys a huge doll for Mrs Poulter, this simply gives him the opportunity to add Mrs Poulter to his catalogue of distrust:

So he got to resent Mrs Poulter, and everyone else who made mysteries as the Peace declined. He began to hate the faces leering and blearing at him in the streets. He hated, in retrospect, Crankshaw and his priests. He hated his brother Arthur, although, or perhaps because, Arthur was the thread of continuity, and might even be the core of truth. (p. 187)

Later on, when the brothers both had dogs, he hated Arthur's dogs, although one was technically his own. He hid from visitors, from his old friend Johnny Haynes who came with his wife to visit him, 'So it was only natural he should continue hating Haynes, clopping like a stallion with his mare all round the house, staring vindictively at it from his barbered eyebrows. . .' (p. 190). When his brother Arthur, who in his strange, stumbling way, has picked up a taste for books, visits the library and is discovered by Waldo, Waldo expels him from the library as a stranger: ' "You will leave this place, please, at once," Waldo commanded in a lower voice. "Please," he repeated, and added very loudly: "sir" ' (p. 201).

There is an unbroken connection between the beginning of the novel, when we see the two neglected, aged men, 'sidling brittly down the path' for their walk out in the dangerous country – dangerous above all to Waldo, since people *lived* in it – and the final, horrifying scene in which Waldo, yielding finally and absolutely to the hatred which he has directed at all living things, is destroyed himself in his effort to destroy whatever he is capable of destroying in Arthur. Dead, deserted by the appalled Arthur, he is locked into the room with the dogs who eat his throat and genitals.

George Steiner, who has noted in White 'the thread of hysteria underneath the dreary crust', remarks how in almost every one of White's novels and short stories there is 'an eruption of savagery'.[5] Certainly there is savagery in this ending, but it would not be accurate to call it an eruption, since it is implicit in the material, has been prepared for with considerable prudence, and is related to the reader indirectly through the wholesome instrument of Mrs Poulter. Moreover, this savagery is, of course, White's rendering of one of the most profound and constitutive perceptions in his work, that is the co-existence of human malice and human goodness which move in and out of one another like the folds of light and darkness in Arthur's glass taw. However, co-existence is not a simple equilibrium; malice – it is more personal and frantic than just evil or disorder – exists as a settled condition of human life whereas goodness is a flickering and accidental visitation. If his work is deeply stained with a sense of the monstrous and the ugly in life, this is balanced by an intense and powerful concept of goodness. Such goodness, though it may be striven for, cannot be deserved. It is a gift and, as the novels make clear again and again, a gift likely to be found in those regarded as blemished or disgusting or hateful – in this novel, Arthur. The powerful positive effect of Arthur requires the negative horror of Waldo. Waldo sees himself as a crystal core to be held in reserve. Arthur's favourite glass marble, susceptible to light and touch, the image of the troubled, ambiguous soul, becomes by the end of the novel an image of the depths and contradictions of human nature, as it exists in the community, in the family, in a pair of friends, or lovers, or brothers, or in the single individual and stricken soul that Waldo and Arthur together compose.

The Vivisector (1970) shows White at the height of his powers, displaying a glittering constellation of gifts. In substance and orchestration it relates to *Riders in the Chariot*: in manner to *The Solid Mandala* and the short stories. The centre of the novel is still, as in *The Solid Mandala*, access to reality by means of neglected modes of consciousness. In this case the mode is examined through an intensely conceived and powerfully realised experience of the art of painting. Hurtle Duffield is born to a family below even the bottom rung of respectability. The mother is a laundress, the father a rag-and-bone man and an empty-bottle collector. The tone in which the family and the scruffy home are described is unusually warm and mellow. The reticent, sweet natured, frightened father and the loving, dishevelled, romantic mother, their scrawny children competing for food and comfort, provide for these children, for all the meagreness of their circumstances and the petulance forced on them by their unnatural intimacy, a living and productive context. White conveys with exquisite finesse the mixed nature of the boy Hurtle, on the one hand as an ordinary child, on the other as a potential painter of genius.

He causes us to feel Hurtle's occupying of an ordinary child's tip-tilted and dramatic universe where touch, and supremely the mother's touch, is all important, validating the child's own existence and helping him to enter the lives of others; where life is insistently and brilliantly in the foreground and the moment, and implication, is shadowy and unreal; where neutral bonds and explanations are hateful; and where the child lays down the fundamental grounds of all his future experience both of feeling and thought. In all these respects Hurtle is shown as a conventional, intelligent, working-class boy, but humming throughout is another intimation. In the life of the normal child the experience of touch is succeeded by that of sight, the feeling for textures ousted by the vision of forms as the primary mode of experience. But in Hurtle's case there is a precocious development of sight, a very early and unusually refined sense of colour and shape. Their beaten weatherboard house and straggly self-sown sunflowers did not matter because of 'the two yellows of the sun and the sunflowers playing together, and the sticky green of the wilted leaves' (p. 11). When his mother fought with him, kissed him, and told him 'It's the edgercation that counts' (p. 12) he did not altogether understand what that meant. Nor did he want to. 'Not as the sun and sunflowers were melting together, and he lay against Mumma's white, soapy neck' (p. 13). He loved the shape of the empty bottles his father collected, and he never tired of handling them:

> He loved the feel of a smooth stone, or to take a flower to pieces, to see what there was inside. He loved the pepper tree breaking into light, and the white hens rustling by

moonlight in the black branches, and the sleepy sound of
the hen shit dropping. He could do nothing about it, though.
Not yet. He could only carry all of it in his head. (p. 17)

Just before the monstrous transaction is completed, and he is
sold to the rich Courtneys for £500, against his father's desperate,
unavailing opposition, and with his mother's anguished but
absolute support, he is visiting the Courtney house where his
mother works in the laundry and it is the colours that he is
intoxicated with:

> It was a smaller, mauve room, the furniture in black, with
> streaks of pearl in it. The room even had a kind of mauve
> scent, from a mass of violets, he recognised from the florists',
> in a silver bowl. Shelves of coloured books and photographs
> in posh frames gave the room a used, though at the same
> time, a special look. There was a hairpin on the carpet,
> and in a gold cage a white bird with red beak looking at
> them with cold eye. (p. 25)

This is a splendid example of the novelist's capacity to adopt
the sensibility he is describing. The accuracy of the scoring, the
primary colouring, the simplicity of the phrasing, arrange before
the reader's eye the scene at which the boy stares entranced.
There had been moments when the damp stone laundry at home,
smelling of Lysol and yellow soap, horrified him, and this other
world, existing behind the door covered with felt which divided
the servants' quarters from the rest of the house, fascinated him
with its silence and beauty, 'He touched the shiny porcelain
shells. He stood looking up through the chandelier, holding his
face almost flat, for the light to trickle and collect on it' (p. 31).
When he is finally established in this world, a new member of
the Courtney family, he continues his double life. On one level
he has relationships with the selfish, romantically sensuous and
neurotic Mrs Courtney, with the inarticulate, kindly, shorn-bull
of a man Mr Courtney, and with his new sister the crippled,
hump-backed Rhoda. But at another level he is alone with his
thoughts. At home in Cock Street, the many children and the
constant noise had protected his private thoughts. In the Courtney
house he himself spoke to protect them, asking distracting
questions which he was not particularly interested in getting the

answers to. He did not love Mrs Courtney but he was in love with the way she looked; he loved the big silent house, 'in which his thoughts might grow into the shapes they chose. Nobody, not his family, not Mrs Courtney, only faintly himself, knew he had inside him his own chandelier. This was what made you at times jangle and want to explode into smithereens' (p. 53).

Quickly he learns the new language, the new manners, and the new assumptions, although they are, as much as anything, a disguise and protection for the reality he nurtures within himself. What that reality is he is still unable to define. When he is on a visit to the outback, where he is deeply touched with the marvellous beauty of the country, he realises that like the expert Sid Cupples, who simply knew better than everybody what to do with the sheep, he, too, knows better than everybody, '. . .not that he could have explained what he knew: because he saw rather than thought. He often wished he could think like people think in books, but he could only see or feel his way' (p. 108). Again he saw in his mind the rough-looking sheep. He itched to get his fingers in their wool, for the feel of it. It is on this visit that he is suddenly certain that he is going to be a painter. It is on this visit, too, that he hears a story from Sid Cupples which became to him increasingly significant in his life:

> He told about a possum they had caught on the place during a plague; the homestead roof had been full of possums: 'Pissin' through the ceilin' on to yer plate. Till we tied a bell round the neck of this 'ere animal – see? Soon as 'e run after 'is mates, the mob of possums began ter disappear. It was the blessed bell – see? It was like this possum 'ud gone off 'is nut. Put the wind up the "sane" buggers.'
>
> Sid laughed and laughed at his memory of the bell-possum; but Hurtle was struck cold: by a vision of himself, the last possum on earth, tinkling feebly into a darkness lit by a single milky eye. (p. 111)

The belled possum, the chandelier, the knife, the eye, are some of the dominant images which throng his dreams and his imagination. And while he continues to live the external life of a rich boy, his original family and life sink away, 'What had become of Mumma? he wondered. Though it wasn't in the contract to see her, her cracked hands would return, sometimes as a source of shame, sometimes of agonising tenderness; but mostly he didn't think about her: a laundress was incredible' (p. 168). He goes to school, he visits Europe, quarrels with his sister, is edgy with his new mother, opens his sexual life, but the true and inward reality more and more coheres about these symbols. On one occasion Mrs Courtney, who sometimes has her frantic insights, says to him suddenly, 'You, Hurtle – you were born with a knife in your hand. No,' she corrected herself, 'in your eye' (p. 150).

The first significant part of the novel, then, is devoted to his childhood. His young manhood and his sudden enlistment when the war starts; the war itself and his year after it in Paris, washing dishes at Le Rat à l'Oeil and working in l'Huissier's studio; his return to Sydney, under his old name of Duffield; his break with his family, even with Rhoda with whom, for all their malicious differences, he had an intimate, intuitive understanding – 'because total love must be resisted: it is overwhelming, like religion' (p. 184): all these things are glided over, and we receive no more than a fleeting report on them. The second phase of the novel opens with Hurtle Duffield, returned to Australia, eating limp chips and encrusted fish in Rushcutters Park after an evening spent 'gutting and scaling fish, peeling and slicing potatoes, with spells of the greyer washing-up' (p. 195) at Café Akropolis, Railway Square.

Hurtle Duffield's relationship with the 'coarse, not exactly old, but lust-worn, prostitute', (p. 196) Nance Lightfoot, does not so much begin as erupt, not so much develop as explode. Their love affair begins with a physical collision in the park, it goes on in an atmosphere which is turbid and gross; the sex in it calls up unsavoury but not wholly irrelevant parallels, a slummocky sprawl, feeding time, pig's trotters. Amid all the wallowing and rootling, the reader finds salutary and refreshing Nance's broad fabliau humour and the crackling raciness of the speech in her circle. Here are two tiny examples.

> 'Who was that? he whispered too loud.
> 'The landlady. She was in the trade herself once. But developed varicose veins.'

'Is she decent?' he chattered as they went on bumping their way up the once graceful stairs.

'As a matter of fact', said Nance, 'a cow's arse is decenter.' She nearly bust herself, and because he was joined on to her he reacted equally to their Siamese joke. (p. 190)

Somebody came knocking at the door and she got up as she was, to open. He caught sight of an old biddy in felt slippers holding a pudding basin to her apron.

'What is it, dear?' asked Nance, protecting herself against the draught.

'I thought ter make a puddun, Mrs Lightfoot, but am fucked for fat,' the old woman said. 'Could you loan me a penny or two for suet?'

'A puddun at five in the mornun? You muster wet yer bed, dear.' But she scratched around on the dressing-table and gave the old thing half-a-crown.

'I won't forget. A nice slice of puddun for Mrs Lightfoot.'

'You could light 'er breath with a match any hour of the twenty-four,' Nance said when her neightbour had gone. (p. 193)

And yet there is in the very fleshy, the almost porcine brand of love-making engaged in by Nance and Hurtle (even if its expression suggests intermittently that the sex is being looked at with an observer's disgust at the antics of caged monkeys) a certain psychological propriety. It is to be expected that a prostitute for whom sex is impersonal and mechanically routine, if she is as full-blooded and as much in love as Nance, might naturally fume with sensuality, gobbling like a baby that which she treats with aloof indifference as a worker. As for Hurtle, the spirituality of that part of his nature which his lust feeds and frees is precisely balanced by the rankness of its sensuality. I have my reservations, then, about this phase of the novel: in particular I sense a degree of over-heatedness in the description of the sexual activity which betokens on occasion some flinching distaste in the writer. But I must not allow this hesitation to blur the fact that for the most part the important section of the novel is profusely and powerfully realised. The palpable grossness of the lust carries with it several advantages for the novelist. It preserves the, by no means original, situation of ponce-artist and prostitute-model from the many melting invitations to sentimental disaster implicit in it. Again, it provides a lyrical but unromantic, and strongly convincing celebration of this most significant element of human experience, and it demonstrates once more Patrick White's extraordinary capacity perfectly to embody a whole range of female character, all the way from the thin-blooded, romantic Theodora Goodman to the full, Rubens-like solidity of Nance Lightfoot.

I have stressed this sexual point, perhaps too much, and I may have given the impression that it is unduly isolated or distorted. In fact it is sunk into the whole economy of the novel and subordinated to the primary theme, Hurtle's growth as a painter. Occasionally, it is true, in his striving to grind out the inner relationship of sex to painting in Duffield's life, White puts too much pressure on language and metaphor and edges near to caricature, for example: 'And what he wanted was not the common possessive pross he loved by needful spasms, but to shoot at an enormous naked canvas a whole radiant chandelier waiting in his mind and balls' (p. 215). But this is the weakness of White's strength, which is to compel words by a strongly physical use of language to assume the shapes he is describing, whether these are the overpowering body of Nance, the rocks around Hurtle's shack, the coming alive of Hurtle's talent or the heroism of will he manifests in developing it. In this part of the novel he uses words like paint, in thick layers and swirling forms which communicate in an authentic and moving way the painter's visual impressions, his organising concepts, his grim and often despairing failures, his glimpses of the reality he is pursuing, his few moments of illumination. It is hard to think of another novelist who could with equal success transpose the experience of one art into the medium of another.

Capacity to move is related to authenticity of representation, and in this phase of the novel White traces Hurtle Duffield's complex route from a drained, lethargic state towards creativity and potency with an unfaltering continuity, backing it with the most exact detail of scene, event and motive. Nance is not only Hurtle's partner in love but 'his work; as he had only begun creating her'.

The following day, in his cramped room, a sense of freedom started him whistling and singing, until he realised the wrestling match was on: to recreate the body as he saw it without losing the feel of flesh. He knew, or thought he knew, how to fix the formal outline; perhaps he had already done so. Now he was faced with laying on the colour: the lettuce tones; kohlrabi purple; crimson radish; old boiled swede for the shabbier pockets of skin. (p. 207)

He finds his private situation of ponce and whore repulsive, but it is also the context and provocation to his other, significant life in which Nance assumes very different forms. He sees her possessed of 'the unconscious nobility of some animals, moving intently on felted pads' (p. 213), or at other times as remote and classical: 'He would have to use her in another context: the head with its heavy-hanging coil of hair' (p. 214). He begins with more and more of himself to live the life for which he had been preparing, or been prepared, for years:

Most of the day he now spent steadily painting, still destroying, but sometimes amazed by a detail which mightn't have been his, yet didn't seem to be anybody else's. There were one or two canvases he had dared keep, in which dreams and facts had locked in an architecture which did not appear alterable. When his fingers weren't behaving as the instruments of his power, they returned to being the trembling reeds he had grown up with. (p. 217)

His one anxiety is that his only convincing self may not take over from him at the easel. What he most required from Nance was not her money or even her love, but something else which joined them together on a purer plane to solve 'equations which might have defeated his tentative mind, and which probably never entered Nance's consciousness' (p. 218). By now he had moved out of the city to a shack in the scrub where he had a hard, lean life and saw Nance only intermittently. 'His tactile mind was the part of him he cosseted: encouraging it to reach out, to cut through the web of dew, to find moisture in the slippery leaves, the swords of grass, before the sun had sucked it up' (p. 229).

At a lower level, admitting some nimble social comedy, we

see the founding of Duffield's reputation as a result of his meeting
with the precisely observed, pansy-dealer, Caldicott, who secretly
hoped that his own life might appear a work of art to others,
to which end he collected works of art and kept a gallery in
George Street 'to encourage interesting boors like Duffield whose
bad taste might eventually be excused as genius' (p. 227).
Duffield's minor degree of fashionable success has nothing to do
with his increasing distance from Nance. In so far as he is capable
of loving anything but his art, he loves her, but as Nance remarks,

> 'Nothin is ever what you expect. I never thought I
> would 'uv taken up with a so-called artist I was lookun
> for somethun else I would 'uv done better to 'uv got fixed
> up with some bloke who expects 'is chop at five-thirty 'is
> regular root Saturday because you're married to 'im any-
> way he thinks you are you aren't inside you are free but
> with an artist you're never free he's makun use of yer in
> the name of the Holy Mother of Truth. He thinks. The
> Truth!' (p. 258)

This impressive and disturbing section of *The Vivisector* is
organised round a psychology which assumes that the purity of
Duffield's artistic purpose needs to be liberated and nourished
by the coarseness, toughness and sensuality embodied in Nance.
The grossness of the latter is inversely – but essentially – related
to the fineness of the former. This is a vision very much in keeping
with White's habit of sensibility, which casts experience into
polar dualities. Its success depends on the strength and conviction
with which the two terms of the relationship are presented. At
this stage of the novel the more important of the two is Nance,
and she is a magnificent creation, brimming with life, realised
with completeness and force and splendidly capable of sustaining
the function she is allotted. She is another example in White's
fiction of the doctrine of Henry James: she can be the striking,
figured symbol, because she is 'the thoroughly pictured creature'.
The violence of Nance's end, after it is fully borne in on her
that she can never be anything but secondary to Duffield's vision
of truth, and she is dashed to death on the rocks below Duffield's
cabin, whether by accident or suicide or both, matches the
brutality of her existence and the part, sacrificial and creative,
she has played in the painter's life.

This is a novel of distributed attention; events that do not contribute directly to the formation of Duffield and the constitutive theme are quietly passed by. When we next see the painter sitting on a park bench being talked to – in the way that happens in public places – by a home-going grocer with a sexual problem, he is a successful painter with canvases in the Tate Gallery and the Museum of Modern Art, his work being bought, as he says, like groceries. He is dressed carelessly in expensive clothes; he lives in a house which fits both the gentleman and the peasant in his background: the front has urns and pretensions, the back looks out on an outside dunny and a slum, a place not only packed with people but swarming with subjects. The inhabitants of Flint Street (the front) and Chubb Lane (the back) consider him an acceptable crank. During these years he leads almost a hermit's life, feeding on bully-beef, bacon and egg, seeing no one, totally independent, compulsively painting.

This next structural division, taking Duffield from his conversation with Mr Cutbush to his middle-fifties, is like the first (his real mother, Mrs Courtney and Rhoda) and the second (Nance Lightfoot), again dominated by women. Indeed, it may be that the remarkable energy generated in White's portrait of the painter may be the consequence of his conceiving it as friction or a quarrel between reality and life – thought of as female – and art and talent – seen as implacably, self-centredly male. There are, however, significant differences between this part of the novel and the one before. To begin with, there is a difference in the tone of the current Hurtle's character from the one we saw being developed under Nance's influence. That perceptive masturbator, Mr Cutbush, notices it when he observes something 'mild and reconciled in his companion's tone'. In his passages with Nance, Hurtle Duffield is struggling with his genesis as a painter, with the moral and personal agony of giving birth to his talent. In his relationship with Olivia (Boo) Davenport, an old friend from childhood, and his Greek mistress, Hero Pavloussi (both, unlike Nance, very rich women), it is Duffield's technical problems in the practice of his art which are more prominent, and if one cannot separate those two orders of difficulty absolutely, there is no doubt that they *can* be separated, and that different weight is deliberately given to him by the writer.

A second significant difference between the Olivia–Hero section and the Nance Lightfoot one lies in the idiom employed: in the former it is sultry and oppressive; in the latter, lighter and clearer, and enlivened by a most engaging wit. It is wit which shows itself in the comic aside, in the dissection of personality, and in the description of things. Perhaps I can best illustrate what I mean by focusing for a moment on one of the brilliant set pieces in this part of the novel, the dinner party given by Olivia Davenport to introduce her friends Hurtle and Hero, 'I'm giving you Hurtle, Hero, for dinner', she says, explaining who is to take in whom:

> There was no sign that a plan had been discussed beforehand by the two women. In fact, Madame Pavloussi, standing in front of him, continued looking dazed, if not frightened, by the possibility that she was intended as a sacrifice; while there flickered briefly through his mind an image of himself trussed on a gold plate, threatened by a knife and fork in her small, rather blunt hands. (p. 326)

Here are two comments in the same good-humoured style about the servants: 'A manservant he hadn't seen before, but who claimed to recognise him, received Mr Duffield at the front door with the virtuoso flourishes of the professional obsequious' (p. 320); 'The majordomo confessed to the hostess in velvety tones that dinner was served' (p. 325); Emily, the elderly maid, half mentor of the family, half honorary nuisance, 'wore the superior, peevish expression of aged servants who have chosen to stay up longer than they are expected to' (p. 342). As well as the wit of comedy and the wit of character, there is also that of description. The two excerpts which follow show description imbued with an urbane, astringent and revealing wit, carrying with it illuminating intimations of temperament. White is describing first Mrs Davenport's dress and then Mrs Pavloussi's:

> She was even wearing a crimson dress, a deep crimson, devoted to the lines of her flanks, her thighs, until the knees, where it began to flounce and froth and lead a life of its own: a bit obvious perhaps, in its effect, if it hadn't been of such a rich, courtly stuff, reminiscent of carnations with a glint of frost on their rough heads. She came forward,

aiming her most stunning smile, trailing invisible streamers of carnation perfume. But the cleverest details of her informally formal *toilette* were the sleeves: these were pushed back to the elbows, in heavy rucks, and although they must have been worn permanently so, she gave the impression of having that moment deserted the sink, her wrists dripping pearls and diamonds instead of suds. (pp. 321–2)

. . .her dress moved with the liquid action of purest, subtlest silk, its infinitesimal bronze flutings very slightly opening on tones of turquoise and verdigris. Again, her miraculous dress was worn with an odd air, not of humility – fatality. It was surprising that, in shaking hands, she appeared to be grasping a tennis racket. Such an incongruous show of strength could have been part of a game she had specially learnt for Anglo-Saxons. (p. 324)

White has a capacity, one he shares with that very different novelist Henry James, for inducing, or perhaps I should say, since it is so fine and nervous a strength, for persuading the amusing to shade into the perceptive, the positively defining touch on character. When, for example, Hero blurts out that it must not be thought her husband will not come to dinner because – he is an invalid or hypochondriac – 'he has a pain in his pinny', the writer comments, 'This echo of an Edwardian nanny cast up on the shores of the Levant started the guests frantically laughing. . .' (p. 322). Or again, Olivia, who has a reputation for being educated and has certainly amassed an exotic token of knowledge, is overheard to remark to a distinguished Orientalist, 'I can't say I *know* Chinese, but confess to four hundred characters' (p. 307).

Olivia (Boo) Davenport and Hero Pavloussi are caught and held with the help of that endorsed discernment which is in part observation, in part projected imagination, which is half experience and half insight. Mrs Davenport, wealthy, twice-widowed, intelligent, devious, both frigid and ambiguous in matters of sex, is drawn with that precise, unerring line invariably used by White on members of the upper class. She is shown encased in a cold, enamelled perfection. 'Like her possessions, whether the white silk she was dressed in, or the stone head of a buddha in a niche, her movements were of a true perfection. She had the most beautifully straight back. Of course Boo Sugar Hollingrake could bloody well afford to be straight-backed and simple' (p. 289). The owner of Klees, a Breugel, a Picasso, a Boudin from Duffield's old home, she 'knows about' painting and her attitude to Hurtle varies from too obvious respect to insolent familiarity. His to her is one of reserved, undeceived and caustic affection. Olivia has the nature of a procuress, and social occasions and assignations planned for her friends were, as Hurtle discovers, the closest she came to sexual pleasure.

Certainly she is the main instrument in the novel – she is in an ambiguous way the lover of both – in arranging in a positive, calculated way, for Hero and Hurtle to fall in with one another, even to fall in love with one another, which they obligingly do. I use the term 'instrument' advisedly about Boo Davenport's function in the novel because she is more than a mere tool or neutral means. She contributes her own thrumming nuance to the musical action of the novel. In the same way, Hero Pavloussi brings to the novel her own complex offering, a mixture of the acrid and the plangent, of the naïve and the Mediterranean. But an instrument is also an inert usable thing. And the tragedy of the relationship of Hero and Hurtle, contrary, fleshy and comically turbulent as it is, appears in the increasing conviction of both that their love is deeply infected by its being an instrument in the passive sense: a fact Hero accepts with despair, Hurtle with resignation,

> . . .he realised he had never been in love, except with painting. He had been in love, he recognised it, with his own 'Pythoness' standing permanently beside the tripod-bidet. This was what made his encounter with Madame Pavloussi – Hero: still a myth rather than a name – of particular significance. He was falling in love with her not in the usual sense of wanting to sleep with her, to pay court to her with his body, which, after all, wasn't love. Physical love, as he saw it now, was an exhilarating steeplechase in which almost every rider ended up disqualified for some dishonesty or another. In his aesthetic desires and their consummation he believed himself to be honest; and in his

desire to worship and be renewed by someone else's simplicity of spirit, he was not forsaking the pursuit of truth. So he was falling in love with Hero Pavloussi. It had begun, he thought, as they stood in front of the Pythoness Olivia Davenport owned; when Hero had innocently planted in his mind the seed of an idea: the octopus thing. (pp. 334-5)

In the final part of the novel Hurtle in his 'dated clothes and corroded mask' has reached a dull, diminished stage in his life when he is at home only with things. They now occupy the position women had in his life, providing subjects, problems of space, technique and colour. But the commodious banality and simple reality of chairs and tables offer insufficient provocation to make his potent vision work. For this women are essential to a sensibility like Duffield's: in the beginning his two mothers and his foster-sister, then a prostitute-wife and a mistress, and finally to complete the range comes the odd, adolescent pianist, Kathy Volkov, whom he feels to be his spiritual daughter. And there is repeated that tincture of incestuousness in his dealing with Kathy that existed in his relationship with Mrs Courtney. He has a grotesque and strained reunion with Rhoda, now a shabby, fretful old woman living with fourteen cats, whom he persuades to come to live with him. Rhoda's feebleness and indifference to her brother's paintings do not blur a point of devastating insight about Duffield's art, ' "Well," Rhoda coughed and smiled, "I might be vivisected afresh, in the name of truth – or art" ' (p. 462).

During the conclusion of his life, Duffield, outwardly 'a cold-eyed elderly gentleman', (p. 540) his emotional life revived by Kathy and Rhoda, continues to wrestle with his demon, to wait for his idea to descend 'out of the clouds into the more practical extensions of space' (p. 362), to play his God-like Vivisector's part, and to paint savage and mysterious pictures.

There was one drawing in which all the women he had ever loved were joined by umbilical cords to the navel of the same enormous child. . .Though they were horrible and frightening, the secret drawings and occasional paintings of this period were what sustained his spirit; even when he couldn't always grasp the significance, he could bask in his own artistry. (p. 540)

The technical problem of this novel is not the presentation of the pictures – these, after all, are objects describable as any others – but the registration of the painter's consciousness and experience, and this is handled with immense skill and flair by a novelist with a notable inwardness of understanding of the art and an equal capacity to render it in words. (It is unavoidable, perhaps, that the descriptions of the paintings should make Duffield out to be an artist of a markedly narrative and symbolic kind.) The real achievement of *The Vivisector* is the marvellous matching of considerable powers with a subject of exceptional difficulty, and the harmonious employment of both to develop a vision of human life in one of its most sensitive phases, which some may take to be cruel but which seems to me implacably accurate and just.

6 The Latest Phase

The Eye of the Storm, appearing just three years after *The Vivisector* and at the end of a fifteen-year series including *Voss, Riders in the Chariot, The Solid Mandala*, seems to imply some theory of continuous literary creation. *The Eye of the Storm* is without doubt worth its place in a glittering line. It is a novel and like the author himself, surely (we cannot make about White's work those calm, formal distinctions which Eliot favoured between man and theme, artist and suffering), pre-occupied with death. This grim and no doubt inescapable infatuation is animated by an incessant, probing inquisitiveness. What exactly does that ancient lady, Elizabeth Hunter – dying in state in Centennial Park, in Sydney, lapped by the care of nurses, servants and lawyers, and the fear and hatred of her own family – feel, and how, and why? The hunger to know is joined in White's novels with the appetite to illustrate, and each is more than gorged In this unflaggingly energetic story of domination, possession, jealousy, love and savagery, which is at once expansive, sending out long sensitive feelers to the Australian country, to France and England, and almost classically concentrated, a handful of Elizabeth Hunter's connections constituting the dramatis personae and their relationships to the plot.

White's power to refine from the grossness of a condition, the subtlety of a mental state has the fullest scope in this recreation of decrepitude and dying, a process into which Mrs Hunter pours more vitality than agitates the whole lives of most people. Her character and situation are beautifully designed to figure White's vision of death as an intense specification of life. This extraordinary woman, surpassingly beautiful when young, had even at seventy a supple body capable of love. People followed dolls and then jewels as her choicest possessions:

111

'When I was a child, Mary, living in a broken-down farmhouse, in patched dresses – a gawky, desperately vain little girl,' Mrs Hunter's eyes glittered and flickered as she flirted with the fringe of her stole, 'I used to long for possessions; dolls principally at that age; then jewels such as I had never seen – only a few ugly ones on the wives of wealthier neighbours; later, and last of all, I longed to possess people who would obey me – and love me of course.' (pp. 161–2)

She herself had never been possessed by anybody, least of all by her treacherous children or mild husband, except occasionally for procreative purposes. Her gift of clairvoyant malice tests the characters of others more shrewdly than the events or crises of their lives. Compassion, she felt, was something one can drown in. But she is much more than superficially cruel. Manipulation of others is a function of the ferocity with which she lives and a kind of purity and disinterestedness with which she serves herself, the vessel of life. 'Only mother was capable of slicing in half what amounted to a psyche, and expecting the rightful owner to share' (p. 404).

White, who has shown himself elsewhere, in *Riders in the Chariot* and *The Solid Mandala* in particular, as deeply disturbed by the cruelty of communities with their inveterate bias in favour of the average, appears in this novel as appalled by the savagery of individual selfishness. Especially is this so of the children, of the fully realised Dorothy, Princesse de Lascabanes, *notre petite Australienne* in France, *bloody foreign woman* in Australia, and the equally firmly grasped theatrical knight, Sir Basil, incestuous (as they become) vultures, visiting to tear at the dying eagle. The force of despair and horror in the novel, to be gauged by the obtrusive presence of pus and excrement, is only lightly relieved, by the kindly, dead husband Alfred and the desperately clumsy nurse, Sister Mary de Santis. Indeed, the book's strongest and most vibrant value, against which I suppose we are to measure the distortions of life, is not virtue in the conventional sense in which it exists in the husband and the nurse but rather the absolute intensity of life represented by Mrs Hunter herself, and perhaps supremely in her dying.

Point had been given to Mrs Hunter's life by an entranced

experience of pure existence she had undergone in a typhoon on an island off the Queensland coast, when she had entered the very eye of the storm. This model or shape of perfection was what she struggled to make the act of dying conform to, in spite of the intervention of human greed, guilt or simple fussiness. It is the inwardness and conviction with which this effort is communicated which raise White's account of her death from pathology to poetry.

As well as the powerful treatment of the central theme, death as the point of life, an exploration of *'ce pays si lointain et inconnu'*, there are other, expected Whitean qualities. There is, for example, the devastating definitions of the minor characters, from a euphoniously named French aristocrat to an Australian dike called Snow Tunks. There is the mockery which brings decisively to heel Australian airs and British graces. There is the strange empathic sense for things and vegetation. There is a gift for luminous generalisation. On the other side there is – though less frequently than before – the syntax bowled disconcertingly off the wrong foot, and there are passages which are too worked, too thick, too opaque. But these things might be found, at least separately, in other writers. What makes Patrick White unique in the contemporary novel in English is his power to discover and present in the grubbiness of life, in the wretchedness of senility in this novel, the depths and distances which Wordsworth found in the life of childhood.

As I have suggested before, growth from a cell or centre, an organic biographical line of movement rather than a plot or more calculated arrangement, is the favoured kind of progression in White's fiction. Thus in *The Eye of the Storm*, although the present is strongly emphasised, and there is a structure which might pass for a conventional plot – i.e. the pattern composed by the children's scheme to get their mother's affairs in order, by which they mean stopping her wasting the inheritance, exacting money and dumping her in an old people's home – the author's concentration on the family, and the opportunity offered by the dying woman's memories to introduce the past, the very active past, are another way to produce the same effect. Moreover, the family setting, evoked with masterly clarity and assurance, fits in with another habit of White's sensibility. His disposition is to go back, to investigate and uncover the depths and wells of human action, an aim at once simple and difficult, but not, I hasten to add, at all like the reductive, psychoanalytic detection of other contemporaries. White's purpose is not to offer an explanation but to recreate the actuality. And for this purpose nothing provides material so rich and suggestive as the family. Again, another marked characteristic of White's mature fiction is the combination of range and intensity, a blend which the Hunter family – with its Australian roots, its multiple European connections, its varieties of temperament, aspiration, failure, and with its central figure, the fiercely intense and absolute Mrs Hunter – offers in a positively prodigal way.

Perhaps I could take up this pair of terms, range and intensity, once more. The strongest impression the reader gets from this novel, in this representative of White's best fiction, is an impression of teeming life and of the focused imagination responsible for it. This applies not only to the sheer multiplicity of characters but even more to the quality of their existence on the page. Each one appears armed with his living credentials and presenting his vital, truly vital, statistics. As Henry James said of Balzac:

> The figures he sees begin immediately to bristle with all their characteristics. Every mark and sign, outward and inward, that they possess; every virtue and every vice, every strength and every weakness, every passion and every habit, the sound of their voices, the expression of their eyes, the tricks of feature and limb, the buttons on their clothes, the food on their plates, the money in their pockets, the furniture in their houses, the secrets in their breasts, are all things that interest, that concern, that command him, and that have, for the picture, significance, relation and value.[1]

White's penetrating and enlivening intuition is enlarged by a nearly boundless faculty of understanding to cover a whole stretch of human temperaments and conditions. There are two other points made in James's essay on Balzac which are also – I once thought 'surprisingly' but no longer do – highly appropriate to White's achievement. First, his vitalising and catholic power is used in an atmosphere – a 'light' as James puts it – which is rich and thick, 'a mixture richer and thicker and representing an absolutely greater quantity of "atmosphere" than we shall find prevailing within the compass of any other suspended frame'.[2] And secondly, White's plan, like Balzac's, was 'to handle, primarily, not a world of ideas, animated by figures representing these ideas; but the packed and constituted, the palpable, proveable world before him. . .'[3]

Let me now illustrate with a few brief and necessarily disconnected instances the width of White's authority over this packed, proveable and sultrily lighted world. Here, for example, is how Elizabeth Hunter, at the age of seventy, appeared to Sister de Santis, a nurse in whom spiritual aspiration is joined to a sensual craving for physical beauty:

> Her face would certainly crinkle under the influence of impatience or anger, but only, you felt, to become the map of experience in general, of passion in particular. Untouched by any of this, her body had remained almost perfect: long, cool, of that white which is found in tuberoses, with their same blush pink at the extremities. If it had not been for professional detachment, the nurse might have found herself drugged by a pervasive sensuousness as she helped her patient out of the bath and wrapped her in towels, during her 'illness'. (p. 166)

This passage, making a clean and salutary contrast with the geriatric horrors surrounding it, constructs a body which is solid, measurable, dimensioned, but which is also a vessel, cool, white, untouched, a vessel, an object of devotion both on the part of Sister de Santis, a devout nurse of 'opulent obsessions', and, we feel, of the owner herself. Here, indeed, is a reality existing in a packed and constituted world and one given its significance, relation and value. An experience comparable in meaning, but appropriately thicker and grosser, is given in the lines when Sir Basil, stuffing himself with a pound of cooked prawns, is sitting on a bench in the Botanic Gardens:

> Sir Basil had no worries, or not for the moment; he was enjoying vegetable status in the city to which he no longer belonged. So he dragged down his tie. And stuffed in some more of the prawns. Around him the fortified soil, the pampered plants, the whiffs of manure, the moist-warm

air of Sydney, all were encouraging the vegetable existence: to loll, and expand, fleshwise only, and rot, and be carted away, and shovelled back into the accommodating earth. He closed his eyes. He loved the theory of it. The palm leaves were applauding. (p. 272)

The cultivated, unnatural ripeness of the vegetation is a suitable setting for one like Basil Hunter in whom scruple and spirit are lapsing back into a spoilt, impervious rankness. Basil the Knight, like his sister Dorothy the Princess (and how acridly present White makes the insolent assurance of the enervated aristocracy Dorothy has married into, as well as the stale flavour concentrated in the family salon, among 'the painted furniture, the faded tapestries, and mould' (p. 55), had been capable of perception before it 'retired behind a legerdemain of technique and the dishonesties of living' (p. 273), and White shows himself quite as effective in presenting characters in whom technique and the dishonesties of living had not worn away perception. The same intimate and particularising style which developed Basil and Dorothy, the corrupt politician, the snobberies of the plutocrats, the pathetic crudities of Snow Tunks and her girl friend, Mix, the fluting inanition of the stranded English actors in Bangkok, can produce in Alfred Hunter, mild, vulnerable, unpretentiously virtuous, a human quality and condition of a totally different order. A single detail is sufficient to set up the tone of Elizabeth Hunter's husband and to imply the steadiness and moderation of his nature. 'Under the carriage clock in the library at "Kudjeri", "Bill" Hunter and Arnold Wyburd would sit talking: each had a respect for functional objects such as clocks, telescopes, razors, barometers, as well as for acts of God; often they were content simply to stare into the fire' (p. 253).

Even this handful of references will indicate to the reader something of the scope and scale of White's world, while the clutch of lines adduced in support will suggest with what volume and weight each item in it, whether object, person, form or feeling, is invested.

I turn now to the other of my pair of terms, intensity, and perhaps I can harden this shadowy word by focusing on a single figure, Elizabeth Hunter, the centre and spring of the novel. Mrs Hunter's life is based upon a definition out of which some of White's most powerful fiction germinates. It is that voiced by

Lawrence: 'A thing isn't life just because somebody does it. . .By life, we mean something that gleams, that has the fourth-dimensional quality.'[4] The dying Mrs Hunter who seemed no more than a

> ruin of an over-indulged and beautiful youth, rustling with fretful spite when not bludgeoning with a brutality only old age is ingenious enough to use, was also a soul about to leave the body it had worn, and already able to emancipate itself so completely from human emotions, it became at times as redemptive as water, as clear as morning light (p. 12)

That other side of her nature glittered occasionally in her eyes, 'some at least of their original mineral fire burning through the film with which age and sickness had attempted to obscure it' (p. 14). The gleam, the fourth-dimensional radiance of pure being this monstrous woman aspires to, 'a state of mind she knew existed, but which was too subtle to enter except by special grace' (p. 16) is 'that state of pure, living bliss she was now and then allowed to enter' (p. 24). It is spoken of as though in a parable by a solid Dutch captain, a fellow passenger of her daughter Dorothy in a plane struck by turbulence:

> 'Some years ago I was at sea – master of a freighter,' the Dutchman was telling in his matter-of-fact, stubbornly enunciating voice, 'when a typhoon struck us, almost fatally. For several hours we were thrown and battered – till suddenly calm fell – the calmest calm I have ever experienced at sea. God had willed us to enter the eye – you know about it? the still centre of the storm – where we lay at rest – surrounded by hundreds of seabirds, also resting on the water.' (p. 71)

Elizabeth Hunter is searching for death in the same spirit in which she sought the eye of the storm, in the (one must call it) mystical experience she has during a characteristically destructive visit she pays with her daughter to a remote island holiday home. She is caught in a violent storm. The storm is magnificently realised, with a Conradian energy and insight, as is the centre of tranquility, the point of tense, creative peace, she finds or enters into:

All else was dissolved by this lustrous moment made visible in the eye of the storm, and would have remained so, if she had been allowed to choose. She did not feel she could endure further trial by what is referred to as Nature, still less by that unnaturally swollen, not to say diseased conscience which had taken over during the night from her defector will. She would lie down rather, and accept to become part of the shambles she saw on looking behind her: no worse than any she had caused in life in her relationships with human beings. In fact, to be received into the sand along with other deliquescent flesh, strewn horsehair, knotted iron, the broken chassis of an upturned car, and last echoes of a hamstrung piano, is the most natural conclusion. (p. 425)

White makes this spiritual experience of an immoral and selfish woman totally convincing. It is for her, as art was for Hurtle Duffield, and neurosis for Theodora Goodman, and the desert for Voss, the entrance to a supreme reality. It gives point to her existence and it is the expression of a kind of genius in her. It is her form of the uniqueness of humanity, and it is this in its various shapes and instances that White's fiction attempts to express. In this novel, the attempt is quite movingly successful.

A Fringe of Leaves, which appeared in 1976, is a novel based both on the history of Mrs Eliza Fraser who was shipwrecked on her husband's brig off the southern end of the Great Barrier Reef in May 1836, and on the accretion of legend around the record. After the Jacobean drama of *The Eye of the Storm*, *A Fringe of Leaves* appears to derive from a part of White's nature descended from Jane Austen rather than John Webster. Its opening is low key in tone; it is more severe in diction, more disposed to social, as it is more objective in moral, analysis. It is also a tighter, more enclosed novel – in spite of the vast geographical span covered – each phase of the action defined by a formal, containing line: by a Cornish farm, an English manor, a ship, a boat, an island, the conventions of an Aboriginal tribe. The composition is organised round the idea of a voyage – not a voyage out but a return voyage. The Roxburghs are returning from Australia, the husband returning to the remaining member of his family, his brother Garnet, the wife returning from her adopted to her original nature, the convict returning to the place he escaped from, life itself returns to its sources.

Another feature of the design is the delicate insistence with which a single phrase, *a fringe of*, is stitched again and again at critical points throughout. There is a fringe on the mazy shawl with a leaf pattern which Ellen Gluyas, the farm girl, is given to signal her new status as Mrs Roxburgh; it is this fringed shawl she draws tight across her bosom as she waits for Garnet Roxburgh, her husband's brother, in the scene in which each seduces the other; it is the fringe of her shawl which the infatuated cabin boy Oswald Dignam warns her is trailing over the gunnel to begin their sensitive relationship; it is the fringe of her shawl she dips in the rock pools after the wreck to suck up the precious water; it is a fringe of leaves the Aboriginal women dress her in after tearing off her ordinary dress; it is this fringe of leaves she conceals her wedding ring in, and it is this fringe she finally loses when she stumbles half dead, naked, into the Oakes's farm after her rescue from slavery by the convict Jack Chance. I should add that the fringe is not a 'symbol' with an abstract one-to-one correspondence, of the sort we have been accustomed to have excavated for us in recent years. It is a natural image, natural in a domestic context, cloudy, intricate and mobile, and carrying a whole set of intuitions and suggestions, hints both of comfort and desperation, of settled convention and the tattered ends of experience.

The novel opens with a scene in which the formality of language and address is matched by a strict formality in the structure, when Mr and Mrs Merivale and her companion Miss Scrimshaw, a lady with Connections, are bidding goodbye to the Roxburghs as they sail from Sydney. They are, says White, 'like minor actors who have spoken a prologue' (p. 24) before they take themselves off into the wings. In this short scene each member of the trio is delineated with the most practised and informative hand: Mr Stafford Merivale engaged by the Crown as a surveyor (like the founder of White's own family in Australia) was of 'that stamp of English gentleman, not so gentle as not to be firm, not too positive, yet not altogether negative, who will transplant reliably from his native soil to the most unpromising pockets of the globe' (p. 10); the vulgar Mrs

Merivale blooms in her attachment to the well-bred Miss
Scrimshaw, and when she sees below the hem of her friend's
mantle a discarded skirt of her own she is at once rewarded by
glimpses of her own generosity; poor Miss Scrimshaw, ' youngest
of a clergyman's protracted family' called Decima by her parents,
'whether out of wariness or cruelty' (p. 15), has a more
complicated nature. It is she, their conversation reveals, who
discerns in Mrs Roxburgh some unravelled secret or mystery,
the mystery which is indeed at the heart of the novel. ' "Ah,"
Miss Scrimshaw replied, "who am I to say? I only had the
impression that Mrs Roxburgh could feel life had cheated her
out of some ultimate in experience. For which she would be
prepared to suffer, if need be" ' (p. 21).

Dramatic in structure – how naturally the story falls into
acts and scenes – poetic in telling, though with a somewhat drier
poetry than the luscious norm, and endlessly probing for some
missed or missing metaphysical or religious truth: these marks
of the other novels are very positively present in *A Fringe of
Leaves*. There is, as well, symmetry between the English material
on the one side, Mrs Roxburgh's hard life with a drunken father
on the crude Cornish farm, and then the gentility which absorbs
her when she gratefully marries their convalescing lodger, the
invalidish Mr Roxburgh (as he continues to be called by his wife);
on the other, the bourgeois patterns of Sydney and Hobart and
the Australia of convicts, assigned servants and Aborigines. In
between them the dividing sea, Captain Purdew's ship, *Bristol
Maid*, and the isolated cabin in which the two Roxburghs write
up their journals, Mr Roxburgh's (morocco-bound) one of the
two poor examples of his creativeness (the other is remodelling
his wife into a provincial English lady), in which any spontaneous
utterance is likely to be erased on reflection; Mrs Roxburgh's,
slightly mis-spelt, written in her 'improved, but never altogether
approved hand' (p. 69), a mask or shawl for what really agitates
her. 'A lonely childhood, followed by marriage with a man twenty
years her senior, had inclined her mind to reverie. Perhaps her
most luxurious indulgence was a self-conducted tour through the
backwaters of experience' (p. 27).

One cannot but be struck by the professional subtleties of
the novelist shown in this work, a matter apt to be overlooked
with a sensibility so positive and dominant as Patrick White's.

The use of the diaries for the purpose of defining the linked and confused territories of sincerity and self-deception is one such. Another lies in the difference of tactic with which the characters are made present to the reader. The less important, for example Garnet Roxburgh, are seen in vivid particularity and are given a markedly physical description. Captain Purdew, is another example, the very starch of whose character as seaman and commander dissolves in the storm, who appears to Mr and Mrs Roxburgh like this:

> From their perch they sat looking back at the one who had them in his keeping, and who, they hoped, was possessed of benign wisdom and super-human powers in spite of resembling an old, moulted member of the same species, Adam's apple wobbling above a dirty collar, blue-red flesh thinly stretched over such bones as were visible, and deposits of salt on drooping lids and in the corners of disillusioned eyes. (p. 174)

Garnet Roxburgh, to whom Mrs Roxburgh is attached by a mixture of sensuality and detestation, parades in addition to aggressive health and spirits, 'the assured insolence of a lapsed gentleman', in his 'cleft chin [and] rather too full, lower lip' (p. 32). We are given fainter physical clues to Mr Roxburgh himself, 'his face was sallow, fine-featured, a glint in the deep-set eyes implying fever, or fretfulness, or both' (p. 26), his 'features refined by sickness to an unnatural perfection. . .' (p. 182). 'Moods and any tendency to animal spirits had been discouraged from an early age by nurses, governesses and tutors on orders from the mother, who feared that too much of either might aggravate his delicate health' (p. 147).

> Fascinated by so much of what he observed in life, whether beautiful or incongruous, he might have made use of it creatively had his perceptive apparatus not been clogged with waste knowledge and moral inhibitions. He would often isolate a form, or tremble with excitement for an idea, as though about to throw upon it a light which would make it indisputably his. Then, instead he drew resentful, or angry, sometimes even ashamed at his presumption (pp. 145–6)

Austin Roxburgh was a man whose religious faith was the product of his respect for his parents. He was much more governed by abstract principles than anything so virile and unqualified as faith. He loved according to the rules of honour and reason but hardly even according to the dialectic of feeling. One would call him austere but that he lacked the force such a term implies. He is a melancholy rather than a tragic figure, whose self-absorbed, attenuated and self-disgusted life is rendered with exquisite fineness and judgement.

All we are told of a physical kind about Ellen Roxburgh is that she was a woman of medium height, about thirty years of age, who parted her hair straight and had a dark complexion, grey-blue eyes and a mouth of masculine firmness. But the whole novel is devoted, with irony and tenderness, to establishing the presence of her character, which on a scale extending from Theodora Goodman to Nance Lightfoot lies somewhere in the middle, in the proximity, say, of Amy Parker, or even perhaps of Amy's husband Stan, with whom she shares a kind of human centrality and like whom she endures a painful struggle towards self-knowledge.

At any given moment, at each stage in her development, White, with a genuine novelist's double discernment, is able to fix the subtlest nuance of her individuality, and with an equal skill and assurance, place it solidly in the social world. This is so whether we see her as a Cornish girl with burnt face and engrossed in country matters, helping her curmudgeonly father to take a heifer as far as Tremayne, or at the same time in her life nursing their sickly lodger Austin Roxburgh and feeling both his social inferior and 'much older, wiser than this slant-stick of a gentleman' (p. 57). Or at the other extreme, after the wreck and the destruction of the party, when she is seen as a slave spontaneously sharing in the elaborate religious rites of her Aboriginal masters, and grasping 'that most of her life at Cheltenham had been a bore, and that she might only have experienced happiness while scraping carrots, scouring pails, or lifting the clout to see whether the loaves were proved' (p. 286). Or again, this is true of life on board before the disaster where we see the sailors accepting the imported social order implied by the Roxburghs, balancing it against the natural authorities in the ship, in a system which shows its own secret tensions, and a Captain superannuated and hollow in emergency. Or again, in the scenes in Tasmania at Garnet Roxburgh's property Dulcet, where Ellen Roxburgh's natural sensuality finds an occasion for fulfilment, when, as she remembers it – but not in her hypocritically innocuous journal – 'if she had been drawn to a certain person it was because some demoniac force had overcome her natural repulsion' (p. 133); and where this new vaulting sexuality of her nature is set in an utterly convincing context of provincial manners, eighteenth-century squirearchy, and the brutalities of a penal settlement.

In the eyes of her husband, a thin, dry, suffering personality, dominated by his mother and his brother, Ellen Roxburgh combined the qualities of both, 'He believed he found them united in his wife, whose sense of duty did not prevent her lips tasting of warm pears' (p. 149). He saw her, too, as 'the brittle work of art he was creating, the glaze of which might crack were she to become aware of her creator's flaws and transgressions' (pp. 202–3). But as Ellen waits on *Bristol Maid* as the storm mounts, she finds one of her great luxuries is simply to be alone and to give up the many-faceted role she had been playing, a loyal wife, tireless nurse, courageous woman, expectant mother, and, she admitted to herself though not to her journal, compliant adultress. She realised that there were ancient, Cornish elements in her nature, secretive and devious, such as she recognised in one of the officers, Mr Pilcher. She was still to some extent a lump of a country girl and no amount of cunning or cultivated self-deceit could abolish that in her. The truth about Mrs Roxburgh, which she begins herself painfully to appreciate, is that she is torn between reality and actuality. That intelligent spinster, Miss Scrimshaw, at the beginning of the novel notes something enigmatic and inexplicable in her. She had always been deprived of some ultimate in experience, and the novel records the efforts of an ordinary, good, sensitive but not particularly talented woman, to come closer to what she had missed and to be prepared to suffer in her pursuit of it. Life itself constantly intervened to block her. The inadequate affection between herself and her husband rules out love in a creative sense; her nature and intellect make faith in the rational man simply an artificial affectation for her. Her suffering in the wreck and the scrub enrich her but give no final answer. Her rescue seems in the end to be a voluntary return 'to the prison to which she had been sentenced, a lifer from birth' (p. 359).

The events of the novel, the crises of her experience, make up a full register of a convincing human life, and Ellen Roxburgh's constant search for some intensity of being gives point and dignity to, as it confirms the strength and reality of, her humanity. She accepts in the end the modest consolation offered by Miss Scrimshaw, 'I expect we shall make our blunders, but would you not say that life is a series of blunders rather than any clear design, from which we may come out whole if we are lucky?' (p. 392). There is a species of modesty in this conclusion suited to the ordinariness of Ellen's nature. But it is also a nature, the novelist convinces us, like any human nature, capable, or at least desirous of, a reality beyond the ordinary run of experience. 'Had the walls but opened at a certain moment, she might even have turned and run back into the bush, choosing the known perils, and nakedness rather than an alternative of shame disguised' (p. 392).

I find *A Fringe of Leaves* one of the most satisfying achievements in White's *œuvre*. The distancing in time, the immaculate historical sense, the lithely moving narrative, the firmly framed and validated universe, the acceptability of the central character, the rich and lucid design, make for an effect of maturity and calm. In most of his novels Patrick White uses some deviation from the norm – it may be eccentricity, neuroticism, disfigurement, genius, violence of the will or feeling – to make the figure who will project the essential experience of the work. Ellen Roxburgh is superbly ordinary and her importance is to embody one of, perhaps the, constituent convictions of White's art. This novel develops and makes explicit, presenting and confirming it not as abstract doctrine but grounded belief, the idea that man must have, as Lawrence put it, a religious connection with the universe. Like Lawrence, White is concerned to open to the modern consciousness the neglected springs of life, the sources of a full and kindled consciousness, in separation from which the soul is crippled and incomplete. His purpose is to demonstrate, or rather to render in the terms of art, the essential religious connection which man must have with life. 'Religious' may be an odd term to use for one who has written so scorchingly about religion and religious people as White, but 'religious', stripped of sectarian sacking, seems to be the only word adequate to White's intention. Lawrence put it like this:

> And I do think that man is related to the universe in some 'religious' way, even prior to his relation to his fellow man. And I do think that the only way of true relationship between men is to meet in some common 'belief' – if the belief is but physical and not merely mental. I hate religion in its religiosity as much as you do. But you, who like etymologies, look at religion. Monism is the religion of the cut-off, father-worship is the cult of the cut-off: but it's the cut-offness that's to fault. There is a *principle* in the universe, towards which man turns religiously – a *life* of the universe itself. And the hero is he who touches and transmits the life of the universe. The hero is good–your own effort is heroic – how else understand it? It's only this image business which is so hateful. Napoleon was all right: it was the Emperor that was out of gear.[5]

The severence of this religious connection with the life of the universe produces, White's fiction is designed to show, disorder in man's psyche and disharmony in his surroundings, soiling what Lawrence himself called in a phrase that White himself might well have used, 'the clarity of being'.

7 *A Rare Talent*

The award of the Nobel Prize to Patrick White in 1973 signalled a new phase in the development of contemporary literature in English. It was the public recognition that a distinguished, indeed a major, talent had arisen in a literary tradition outside that of Britain and the United States. Whatever one thinks of the Nobel Prize, and some of its recipients are certainly startling, this was undoubtedly an event of unusual significance. It raised, incidentally, the question as to whether one could advance the name of a modern British novelist who might conceivably be a candidate for the Nobel Prize. There are indeed some fine novelists in Britain, but I would find it hard to suggest one of the quality and largeness of creative achievement which one must suppose to be the requirement for the award of the Nobel Prize. If we look for energy, creative energy, in the novel, it seems to me that we have at present to go outside Britain. It is, indeed, energy which characterises so much in the work of Commonwealth writers, and perhaps above all which characterises the creative insouciance and such sumptuous imagination of Patrick White. The sense of a more inhibited life which the reader finds in his writings and in so much other Commonwealth work, comes, I suppose, from a more substantial, if not necessarily better grounded, confidence in the future, which is itself related to a more aspiring and more buoyant national purpose than we know in Britain.

A serious novelist cannot but be involved in accumulating the spiritual experience of the race. He is concerned to draw the exact curve, the specific sensibility, of his own time and nation. He is the analyst and critic of his society. And if he is a Commonwealth novelist, and an Australian novelist like Patrick White, he is doing these things with the powerful pressure of

126

English Literature removed some way from him. He is, to some degree, free from the suffocating conviction that it has all been done before and so much better. Not that one thinks immediately of Patrick White as an Australian novelist, although Australian experience and the Australian scene figure powerfully in his work, whether it is the Australia of masses huddled in cities on the edge of the continent and devoted to the virtues of suburbia, or another Australia of infinite distances, paradisal light and unimaginable age, an impersonal and mineral Australia which is the apt nurse of heroic virtues. White is very much in the European tradition, of Tolstoy, Dostoevsky, Turgenev and Lermontov, of Dickens and Lawrence, and indeed of that other part of the European tradition in Cowper and Melville. He has been criticised by George Steiner precisely on the score that his novels bring to bear a European sensibility against the emptiness of the Australian context:

> The reciprocities of minute material detail and vast time sweeps, the thread of hysteria underneath the dreary crust, the play of European densities against the gross vacancy of the Australian setting, are the constant motifs of White's fiction.[1]

To me it seems that the force of White's creative capacity, which is itself derived from the double element Steiner notices, is perfectly capable of bringing the duality into something single and harmonious.

Certainly the qualities of largeness, uninhibited confidence, and potent creative energy are present in all White's major works, and particularly in the cycle which includes *The Tree of Man*, *Voss*, *Riders in the Chariot*, *The Solid Mandala*, *The Vivisector*, *The Eye of the Storm* and *A Fringe of Leaves*. In quality and authority these compose an *oeuvre* which suggests a strong and continuing creative power. It is a power which shows itself most vividly in White's use of language. This is of such an individual sort that it stamps the work indelibly with the writer's personality, and it is a form of that characteristic domination of his material which this artist invariably exhibits. White has been castigated by some critics precisely because of this peremptory wrestling with the language. Certainly he allows himself great freedom to ignore many of the common formalities of the tongue, and unusual liberty in dislocating the syntax. Sometimes this can seem clumsy and fabricated; at others, when imaginatively controlled, it becomes an individual and functional skill which adds greatly to the armoury of the novelist.

White's creative power shows itself, too, in the flow of metaphor. The narrative itself is figured and analogical, and many of the novels are themselves sustained by a constitutive and creative metaphor. White's is a sensibility that naturally finds expression in metaphor. In *The Vivisector*, for example, the metaphor at the heart of the novel is art as cruelty, art as the torturer of accepted realities; in *Voss* it is life as the exploration and the human being as the explorer of extremes; in *Riders in the Chariot* it is the heavenly chariot as the intuitive, immediate, poetic and religious consciousness; or the glass marble, enigmatic lights of which mirror the cloudy depths of personality in *The Solid Mandala*.

Such metaphors, with their mysterious connections with the profounder part of human nature, enrich and complicate the fiction. In *The Eye of the Storm*, for example, a fit member of an impressive family of novels, the entranced experience of pure existence which the heroine undergoes in a typhoon on an island off the Queensland coast constitutes a model or shape of perfection that she struggles to make her life, and then the act of dying itself, conform to; and it is an ordering and clarifying influence in the novel, turning what might have been a clinically exact account of disintegration into a more complex, more humanly significant composition. In the same way, neurosis in *The Aunt's Story* becomes the means to an apprehension of reality fuller than the conventionally 'normal' one. And the capacity for decent ordinariness evoked and analysed in *The Tree of Man* is transformed into a higher order of existence altogether, requiring a kind of genius, the genius for stubbornly staying – in Henry James's phrase, 'the subject's truth of resistance'. Art as the knife and the artist as the tormented and disciplined surgeon; life as the unexplored desert, and the extremes of suffering and simplicity as the conditions of man's deepest experience; neurosis as a figure of the effort towards a purer vision; twins as the image of the divided self; the disruption of the common world of substance by the single and singular soul: it is by means of this play of metaphorical life that one comes to have access to White's extraordinarily intense art and to the vision of life which orders and supports it.

It is a vision which we may call religious, poetic and profoundly melancholy, though it is not religious in any specifically Christian sense. It is based on a paradox, the coexistence of human malice and human goodness which flow in and out of one another like the folds of light and darkness in Arthur's glass marble in *The Solid Mandala*. Malice is a settled condition of human life but goodness is a grace, a visitation. These are the facts of human life as White perceives them; the hope, if there is hope, lies in those conditions of simplicity, suffering, misery, by which we may achieve a purer and more disinterested relationship with existence, the conditions shown in the lives brilliantly exemplified in *The Tree of Man*, *Riders in the Chariot*, and *The Solid Mandala*. With such characters, with Miss Hare, Mrs Godbold, Himmelfarb, Arthur, Waldo, this purer relationship is a product of an organ of consciousness in some way independent of experience. It is a gift of insight nourished in privacy, which is recognised by those who themselves possess it and which invariably provokes persecution. White's is a harsh and ravaged reading of human reality in which communities persecute anyone beyond the average, families are torn by hatreds, and individuals wrestle in loathing with others. We find, too, a certain disrelish for life, or for some parts of life, a flinching distaste reminiscent of Eliot in respect of sexual experience, for example. But we are also aware – it may be more obliquely, less positively – in all the novels of the flow of life, of the possibility of illumination, and the conditions under which something rich and healing can be constructed. It takes a talent of a rare order to keep these two themes in place and in proportion.

The communication between the two sides of White's sensibility is continuous and smooth; at least for the most part. It is interrupted on occasion, it is true, by language which is too thick, too opaque, or again, by an excess of explicitness which harks after a gratuitous symbolic symmetry, but in general the more positive qualities of his genius render the Manichaean violence of his version of human relationships with that extraordinary and convincing concreteness which follows when minute fidelity of observation is enlivened by imaginative power.

The range of his sympathies is extraordinary: as responsive to the mercantile society of nineteenth-century Sydney as to the seedy horrors of contemporary suburbia; as open to the prejudices of a nineteenth-century explorer as the spirituality of a saintly Jew; as sensitive to the subtlety and scope of the artist's business as it is to the process of dissolution in an aged woman; as in keeping with the toughness and stamina of central and common human experience as with the disturbing irregularity of mental decay. These sympathies are realised in an art which strives for the palpable, the sculpted, the illustrated, and which is made nervous and tremblingly alive by the novelist's incessant and probing curiosity about every form of human experience and every state of human existence. And they are enlightened by a gift for cogent speculation and by a wit which can be either vivacious or sour. Patrick White is a strongly individual, richly gifted, original and highly significant writer whose powers are remarkable and whose achievement is large. His art is dense, poetic, and image-ridden. It is always a substantial and genuine thing. At its finest it is one which goes beyond an art of mere appearances to one of mysterious actuality.

Notes

Notes for Chapter 1

1 'The Prodigal Son', *Australian Letters*, vol. I, no. 3 (April 1958), p. 38.
2 Ian Turner, 'The Parable of Voss', in *An Overland Muster*, ed. Stephen Murray-Smith (Brisbane, 1965), pp. 71–5.
3 A. A. Phillips, 'Patrick White and the Algebraic Symbol', *Meanjin*, no. 103 (vol. XXIV, no. 4) (1965), pp. 455–61.
4 H. M. Green, *A History of Australian Literature, Vol. II, 1925–1950* (Sydney, 1961), pp. 1045–6.
5 'The Prodigal Son', p. 39.
6 Barry Argyle, *Patrick White* (Edinburgh, 1967), p. 6.
7 R. F. Brissenden, *Patrick White* (London, 1966), p. 14.
8 Geoffrey Dutton, *Patrick White* (Melbourne, 1971), p. 8.
9 Henry James, *Autobiography*, ed. F. W. Dupee (London, 1956), p. 563.
10 Anthony Beal (ed.), *Selected Literary Criticism of D. H. Lawrence* (London, 1955), p. 111.
11 P. Lubbock (ed.), *Letters of Henry James* (London, 1920), p. 305.

Notes for Chapter 2

1 Kathleen Coburn (ed.), *Inquiring Spirit* (London, 1951), p. 204.
2 Aldous Huxley (ed.), *Letters of D. H. Lawrence* (London, 1932), p. 405.

Notes for Chapter 3

1 'The Prodigal Son', p. 39.
2 loc. cit.
3 ibid. pp. 38–9.
4 G. A. Wilkes, *Australian Literature: A Conspectus* (Sydney, 1969), p. 92.

5 James McAuley, 'The Gothic Splendours', in *Ten Essays on Patrick White*, ed. G. A. Wilkes (Sydney, 1970), p. 36.
6 ibid., p. 38.
7 ibid., p. 45.
8 R. F. Brissenden, op. cit., p. 30.
9 Barry Argyle, op. cit., p. 42.
10 R. F. Brissenden, op. cit., p. 36.
11 F. R. Leavis, *The Great Tradition* (London, 1948), p. 29.
12 John Updike, *Picked-Up Pieces* (London, 1976), p. 301.

Notes for Chapter 4

1 D. H. Lawrence, 'Education of the People', *Phoenix*, ed. E. D. McDonald (London, 1936).
2 Kathleen Coburn (ed.), op. cit., p. 68.
3 Barry Argyle, op. cit., pp. 90–107.
4 R. F. Brissenden, op. cit., pp. 41–2.

Notes for Chapter 5

1 D. H. Lawrence (trans.) *Cavalleria Rusticana* (London 1928). Quoted in Anthony Beal (ed.), op. cit., p. 290.
2 Aldous Huxley (ed.), op. cit., p. 405.
3 Kathleen Coburn (ed.), op. cit., p. 68.
4 D. H. Lawrence, 'Education of the People', p. 190.
5 George Steiner, 'Carnal Knowledge', *The New Yorker* (4 March, 1974), p. 109.

Notes for Chapter 6

1 Leon Edel (ed.), *The House of Fiction* (London, 1957), pp. 73–4.
2 ibid., pp. 71–2.
3 ibid., pp. 72–3.
4 Anthony Beal (ed.), op cit. p. 111.
5 Aldous Huxley (ed.), op. cit., p. 688.

Notes for Chapter 7

1 George Steiner, 'Carnal Knowledge', p. 109.

Bibliography

White's Works
All references are to the first English edition.
Novels
Happy Valley (London, 1939)
The Living and the Dead (Toronto, London, New York, 1941; Penguin, 1968)
The Aunt's Story (Toronto, London, New York, 1948; Penguin, 1963)
The Tree of Man (New York, 1955; London, 1956; Penguin, 1961)
Voss (New York, London, 1957; Penguin, 1970)
Riders in the Chariot (London, Toronto, New York, 1961; Penguin, 1964)
The Solid Mandala (London, Toronto, 1966; Penguin, 1966)
The Vivisector (London, New York, 1970; Penguin, 1973)
The Eye of the Storm (London, 1973; New York, 1974)
A Fringe of Leaves (London, 1976)
Short Stories
The Burnt Ones (London, Toronto, New York, 1964; Penguin, 1968)
The Cockatoos (New York, Toronto, 1975)
Plays
Four Plays: 'The Ham Funeral', 'A Cheery Soul', 'The Season at Sarsaparilla', 'Night at Bald Mountain' (London, 1965)
Return to Abyssinia was produced in London in 1947 but no copy survives.
Poems
The Ploughman and Other Poems (Sydney, 1935)
Autobiographical Essay
'The Prodigal Son', *Australian Letters*, vol. I, no. 3 (April 1958), pp. 37–40.

Index